THE CHILTERNS

KEVIN FITZGERALD

THE CHILTERNS

B. T. Batsford Ltd

London

First published 1972

© Kevin FitzGerald 1972

Text printed in Great Britain by Northumberland Press Ltd,
Gateshead, Co. Durham. Plates printed and books bound by
Richard Clay (The Chaucer Press) Ltd, Bungay, Suffolk for
the publishers B. T. Batsford Ltd, 4 Fitzhardinge Street
London W1H OAH

ISBN 0 7134 0074 9

CONTENTS

LIST OF ILLUSTRATIONS

ACKNOWLEDGMENTS

The Author and Publishers would like to thank the following for permission to reproduce photographs: Barnaby's Picture Library (11, 20, 27); J. Allan Cash (10); Robert Glover (16, 17); Noel Habgood (14); A. F. Kersting (4, 6-9, 18, 23-25); Jane Miller (2, 5); Pix Photos and G. F. Allen (19, 21, 22, 26); Kenneth Scowen (*frontispiece*, 3, 12, 13, 15). The jacket, showing the Vale of Aylesbury from Cymbeline's Mount with Ellesborough Church in the foreground, is from a transparency by Picturepoint Ltd.

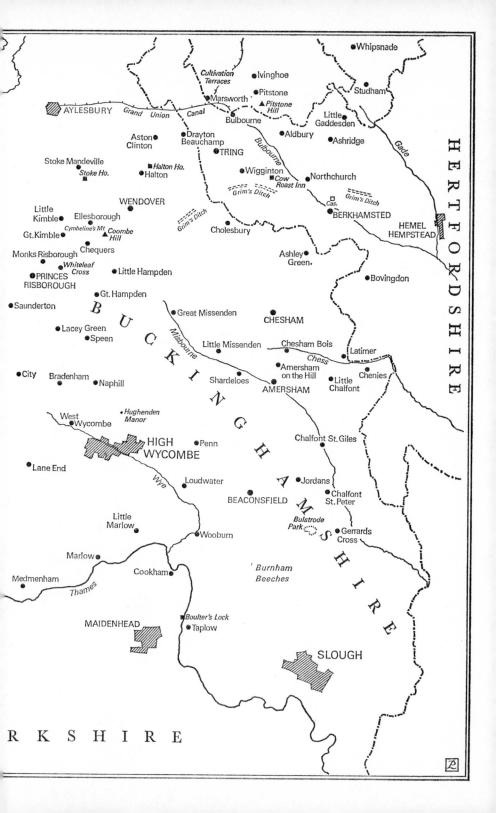

Preface

When a trained historian begins the writing of a book he has already learned what to do as well as how to set about it. Armed with a score of notebooks, and exceptional powers of concentration, he roams through his selected period, picking and choosing, his mind looking forward with pleasure to the scholarly footnotes he will add to his text long before he has faced and settled the problems of style and the story he has to tell.

A 'Chiltern book' cannot be prepared like that. The ground has already been most thoroughly tilled and many crops of books raised from it. The author of a new Chiltern book must read all or most of these, walk about the area a great deal, motor every square mile of it, and of course live in it. A serious history of a single Chiltern village might take ten years to research and write. It has taken over two years to write what is here. And at least six months of reading and conversation.

The people consulted have been more important than the books. For many years the writer has been pestering Miss Evelyn Gibbs of Chinnor, broadcaster and teacher, traveller extraordinary in Africa and elsewhere, to put down on paper her Chiltern reminiscences. She was born in the house where she lives and her forbears have come from around these parts for generations. If there is a titbit of information available in the area bounded by Thame, Princes Risborough, High Wycombe, Miss Gibbs will be able to confirm or deny it. Let there be doubt over some historical aspect of Pulpit Hill; Miss Gibbs will settle it. Let some stranger to the region give the obvious pronunciation to Wainhill and Miss Gibbs will demonstrate where the accents should fall. This book owes a lot to her. And it owes its very existence to Mr. John Aspland, High Wycombe bookseller and personal friend of more than 20 years.

There is a big debt owing to Mr. Ron Siarey, whose profound knowledge of the timber trade and its effect on Chiltern life has been at the service of the writer since the day the work began. Mr. Siarey knows the 'secret Chilterns' as well as he knows the main road to Aylesbury and it was under his aegis that parts of them were 'discovered'.

In 1969 three members of the Chinnor Parish Council, all of them friends, published a short study, 'Youth and Leisure in the Chilterns' which has been of the greatest assistance, not so much in the extraction of information but in the steering of my thoughts towards what was and is happening all over the Chilterns. To Doctor B. L. E. C. Reedy, Mrs. Heather de Freitas, J.P., and to Mrs. D. P. Tucker, I express my thanks.

Mr. George Ordish, who knows a great deal about almost everything, was early on the scene, beginning with many pages of relevant photostat from Camden's *Britannia* of 1695; at every stage of the book Mr. A. D. M. Cox, the historian and Senior Fellow of University College Oxford (and President of the Alpine Club), has expressed interest or offered a comment. The short appendix on Lollardry in the Chilterns was inspired by him, but he is not responsible for a word of it.

Mr. John Taylor of Penn helped with the industrial observations (all much shortened, alas, as the work progressed), and provided valuable information about non-British immigration into the area. This is by no means so great as is popularly supposed, occurring mainly around High Wycombe. Much information was also provided by Mr. N. G. Mansouri of the Wycombe and District Integration Committee. It would have been most interesting to have looked at the Chiltern immigration problem in general terms. In High Wycombe alone there are sizeable communities of Italians, Poles, Spaniards, Hungarians, and Ukrainians, as well as the more easily noticeable settlers from Pakistan, India and the West Indies. There is an Islamic Mission in High Wycombe as well

as a Pakistani Welfare Association and a branch of the Commonwealth Peoples' Association. But a study of all that would lie far
outside the empirical limits of this book.

Mr. William Clarke of Chinnor has been an unfailing source
of local information, having himself taken part in some Chiltern
events of outstanding interest. Some years ago the writer was rash
enough to attempt a few notes on the Chinnor Parish Church, of
St. Andrew. The day after the booklet was put on sale in the
church (for the benefit of the Bell Fund), Mr. Clarke's numerous
and invaluable corrections were in the author's hands. Since then
much Chiltern lore has been discussed and digested.

Most of the observations on the Chiltern furniture trade are
based on information provided (when not from Mr. Siarey), by
the author's friend Mr. Geoffrey Gomme, and his cousin Mr. Leslie
Gomme, during a remarkable day at the giant G-plan factory in
High Wycombe, of E. Gomme and Sons Limited. It is an exciting
experience to sit in the office of a Gomme, holding in one's hand a
'Gomme Shilling' almost 200 years old. Chiltern timber may no
longer be the main support of this great enterprise, but Chiltern
timber put it there.

How is a writer to acknowledge adequately the help received
from dozens of unknown incumbents, parish workers, men lean-
ing on gates, ladies out with dogs? There must now be hundreds of
people living in the Chilterns, from Dunstable to the Goring Gap
and from Slough to Thame, who have watched an elderly man in
black glasses groping his way through a lych gate, fumbling at a
church door, peering at a monument. Many of them have pointed
directing fingers up lanes, shaken their heads in doubt, looked
meaningly at offertory boxes. They are all, here, most warmly
thanked.

It is customary to conclude the average short Preface with warm
tributes to a helpful secretary, and a wife. A mass of books, papers,
leaflets, brochures, journals and letters spread deeply but unevenly
and without order over the floor of a writing-room testifies to the
absence of the former; every line of the book to the presence of the
latter. There cannot be a road junction in all the 500 Chiltern

square miles which has not heard the agonised cry, 'Left, I said *left*'. There is certainly no comma which has not been weighed in a balance of judgement and transferred to its rightful place. Were it not that 'Fowler' has explicitly forbidden its use, the phrase 'demonic energy' might well have been applied to the endless domestic readings and checkings essential to the production of the simplest manuscript of a Chiltern kind.

Finally a word of gratitude to Messrs. Batsford and in particular to Mr. Sam Carr who refused to consider the return of a contract when eye operations compelled nearly a year's delay over the book, and a forgiving thought for all the critics encountered during the writing. Here the *Seven Types of Ambiguity* of Professor Empson helps. The answer to the reiterated question of the last two and a half years, 'Why you?', must be sought for good or ill in the pages of this book.

2   *St. Leonard's Church, Watlington*

CHAPTER ONE

The Area Defined

All the Chiltern country may be seen on Sheet 159 of the Inch-to-a-mile Ordnance Survey. There are about 500 square miles of it defined by Professor Coppock as 'the human response to the rock pattern of South-East England, the alternation of scarp and vale, of limestone, clay, sand and chalk resulting in a series of rural landscapes each with distinctive characteristics'. These rural landscapes are to be found in the counties of Buckinghamshire, Oxfordshire, Hertfordshire and Berkshire, with the Buckinghamshire escarpments ever more closely overbuilt as they reach towards London, the Oxfordshire main ridge still sheltering large tracts of heavily timbered unspoilt country, the two other counties being less typical in character but undeniably 'Chiltern' in certain aspects. E. M. Forster thought of the Chilterns as an important part of the body 'of the great chalk spider who straddles over our island, whose legs are the North Downs and the South Downs and the Chilterns, and the tips of whose toes poke out at Cromer and Dover.' There is in fact no feeling of real change in passing out of Bedfordshire from the Dunstable Down country around Pitstone into undoubted Chiltern country at, say, Aston Clinton.

Taken as a whole the Chiltern area is the most densely wooded part of England and until 1950 continued, with the exception of the southern escarpment, to be among the more sparsely populated districts of the country. The soil is everywhere poor, a factor which has always militated against land settlement until the spread into the countryside of urban man.

At the dawn of history an unknown sea washed the Chiltern ridges, and, later, a forgotten Thames. The little summit at Lane

3 *800-year-old birfurcated tower of St. Bartholomew's Church, Fingest*

End, near High Wycombe, is a true marine bench from the Eocene era. But there are surprisingly few indications of early man; some neolithic traces at Princes Risborough; indications of Bronze and Iron Age man dispersed over the hills. This, until now, was always wild and untamed country.

All the known invaders of Britain came to the Chilterns. The Romans found the Icknield Way and, as they developed their road system, improved long stretches of it. Saxons and Danes ravished the entire area and then settled parts of it. The first Normans came into the Chilterns within months of the Battle of Hastings, and it is said that William the Conqueror led his knights into Bledlow after a difficult passage through the hills at the Risborough Gap. Centuries later the Wars of the Roses brought tribulations and executions to the Chilterns, including the deliberate wiping out of some Chiltern-settled families. The first shots of the Civil War were fired in these parts, John Hampden being mortally wounded at Chalgrove Field and dying in Thame. Despite all these events most of the Chiltern villages and hamlets as we know them today are less than a thousand years old, many Chiltern names being post-Norman Conquest and dating from mediaeval times.

The spread of London has marked and scarred a few areas of the Chilterns beyond redemption, but much that is worth preserving remains. There are over 3,000 miles of negotiable Chiltern foot and bridle paths and there is no other part of the country except perhaps East Anglia where it is possible to be so close to the centre of affairs and yet to drive about in comfort on such long stretches of deserted roads. More than a fifth of the entire Chiltern area is still woodland, much of it in the safe hands of the National Trust or of landowners skilled in the practices of beechwood forestry. The beautiful but now almost suburban 'lung' of Burnham Beeches is owned by the City of London. At all times of the year, but particularly in early spring and late autumn, the Chiltern beechwoods are among the glories of England.

Twenty years ago there were fewer grounds for hope about the preservation of the Chilterns than there are today. Some villages, some whole districts, will undoubtedly be 'let go' so that

4   *The tomb of Alice, Duchess of Suffolk in St. Mary's Church, Ewelme*

the area as a whole, now officially defined as 'A.N.B.' (Area of Natural Beauty), will so remain. The whole country has almost overnight become conscious of the dangers threatening the environment, but in the Chilterns it has also been realised that blind opposition to change is unhelpful and that an order of priorities is necessary to establish those battle grounds on which it is feasible to stand and fight. In all such matters the fast growing Chiltern Society is prominent, alongside the C.P.R.E. (Council for the Protection of Rural England), in forming and leading an enlightened public opinion. There will undoubtedly be numerous major building developments in the Chilterns in the decade ahead, but now the probabilities are that these will be landscaped into the countryside and no longer, as in the recent past, be put down in huge blocks on the cheaper sites without regard to the long-term requirements of the incoming populations.

The traditional industries of the Chilterns are based on the woodlands and the chalk. There are 138 furniture factories in High Wycombe, with others in Princes Risborough and elsewhere. The Forest Industries Research Station is at Princes Risborough. There are two great cement works, at Chinnor and Pitstone, and a third on the edge of the territory at Kidlington. Of recent years much light industry has moved into the Chilterns. Until about the time of the First World War the two cottage industries of lacemaking and duck-keeping were great features of the Buckinghamshire Chilterns, but today the bobbins of the lace-making pillows, particularly those with prayers or aphorisms carved into them, are highly priced collectors' items, and there is rarely a duck to be seen.

The post-war population explosion in the Chilterns has produced some staggering problems, often for small parish councils elected to deal (under the Rural District and County Councils), with the trivia of village life, and now finding themselves confronted by sophisticated men of business, by the need to educate hundreds rather than scores of children at primary school level, by the breaking down of water and sewage facilities under the pressures of vast expansion schemes and by the realisation that the

5　*The beechwoods near Hambleden*

roads about them are inadequate for the new traffic brought in by development.

The newcomers to the Chilterns who have created these problems differ greatly from the usual type of commuter-dweller in South-East England. They are not in the main London workers but people prepared to take less money and to hold more modest ambitions in exchange for the benefits of living in a country atmosphere close to their place of work. A man or woman earning their money at almost any kind of work in High Wycombe, Aylesbury, Bicester, Oxford or Banbury can live practically anywhere in the Chilterns and be within comfortable motoring distance of desk or bench. In a recent Chiltern village survey, of 1,000 adult workers 'polled' only 70 went to London each day. Of the remainder, 300 worked in the neighbourhood and the rest in nearby Buckinghamshire and Oxfordshire towns.

There are some who now despair of any real 'country' future in the Chilterns but they are, naturally enough, mostly those living in affected districts. They have taken part in widely supported protest meetings against particular developments which have then been banned by their parish council, backed by the rural district and county councils. They have seen decisions of this unanimous character overruled from Whitehall and yet another 400 or 500 houses set down on the outskirts of their villages, with all the problems of education and the provision of facilities such actions bring in their train. They have seen the M4 extension driven through an unspoilt ridge on a route opposed by every amenity society in the Chilterns, and by nearly every resident, merely because the planners in London have decreed that it should be so. And that in the face of an alternative route which satisfies everyone. But at the back of everything remains the fact that much of the Chiltern loveliness is imperishable, and hundreds of square miles of Chiltern country will still be much as they are now at the turn of this century. From some of the very worst defacements it is still only a matter of a few hundred yards to open country and the quiet beauty of the hills.

It is difficult to think of most of the present-day Buckinghamshire towns as part of the Chilterns, but that is what they are. As recently as 1906 (when the railway came to it), Gerrards Cross was an unknown, unvisited Chiltern village. Amersham-on-the-Hill is younger than that, and it was only between the two World Wars that the Chalfonts became almost a part of outer London. In 1900 there were 6,000 inhabitants in Chesham; the figure now is over 17,000. At the time of the Boer War, Slough was a little market town of 5,000 people and nearby Stoke Poges was still 'far from the madding crowd's ignoble strife'. High Wycombe has always been a separate case, an industrial town with a difference, lying at the very heart of the Chilterns. Wood is a gentle material, not producing spoil heaps, wastelands of scrap metal and rubbish and dangerous effluents. But 25 years ago there were only 17,000 people in High Wycombe whereas now there are more than 70,000.

When later in this book we are looking at some of these Buckinghamshire towns we shall bear in mind that although, as Professor Coppock has written, the whole southern escarpment of the Chilterns is almost irretrievably lost, yet within those mazes of houses, trunk and major roads and endless residential streets, much of beauty and interest survives for our delight. It is still 'leafy Bucks' which comes to mind when the word 'Chilterns' is pronounced, and even the most densely populated of rail routes through it, that from Aylesbury, via Stoke Mandeville, Great Missenden and the Chalfonts to Marylebone will demonstrate all the year round how much of England still remains to be enjoyed.

Even now the Oxfordshire Chilterns, the lovely ridge from Wainhill to Watlington, with its marvellous views all the way, are almost entirely unspoilt, much of the country still being more suitable for walking than motoring. Here the Chiltern hills are at their steepest, the woods at their thickest and most carefully worked. The lines of communication are poor, there being no longer a railway. These things place much of the countryside beyond the ingenuity of developers and exploiters and, let it also be said, perhaps those just as dangerous members of the community who appear to see much of England as potentially a cross between a vast playground and a municipal park.

Watlington, small enough and beautiful enough in its old-fashioned way for anyone, is the only place of any size in the area and, except for Ewelme, no one has bothered to write much about the various hamlets and tiny villages. Their histories are enshrined in the Oxfordshire volumes of the Victoria County History.

There are only two genuine main roads at present in the Oxfordshire Chilterns, the A423 from Henley through Nettlebed, and the A4009 from Reading through Nettlebed. For the rest a network of secondary roads winds about through the woodlands and up and down the hills. It is still quite difficult without occasional references to a map to drive from, say, Berins Hill, above Checkendon, to Christmas Common at Watlington. H. J. Massingham called all this area (Checkendon, Nettlebed, Swyncombe, Stonor, Turville) the heart of the Chilterns and he described Maidensgrove as 'the most remote of Chiltern hamlets'. It is still that. Indeed the Oxfordshire Chilterns are not guide-book country, despite the fact that a personal guide is a great help to the stranger in many parts of them. There is a sameness which never tires, a sameness of steep hill, of lanes and roads, of beechwoods, and of quiet.

The little hills of Berkshire are certainly a part of the Chilterns, but 200 or 300 feet of rise hardly amount to a foothill and the interest of the Berkshire Chilterns is really that of the river towns, the Thames itself, and the less highly developed areas about Reading.

It would have been easier to write of the Berkshire Chilterns and the Chiltern heaths 30 years ago. The motor-car has turned that whole countryside into an easily negotiable and thus unnoticed through route. Cookham and the two Marlows, Maidenhead and Henley are all in the Chilterns, but no one bothers much about the places in between. Windsor was once a Chiltern town, with its own beechwood Chiltern forest, in the remaining royal woodlands of which it is more than probable that the first Windsor chair was made in the middle 1700s. One of the last hand-bodgers of chair-legs is alive near Ascot Heath today. There are no more of them where once they flourished, around High Wycombe, and Chinnor and the woodlands of the Bledlow Ridge. The Chiltern heaths which survive are no longer typical, except for patches around Bagshot and beyond Caversham Park, near Reading.

There remains Hertfordshire and (some would say), a tiny part of Bedfordshire. Here the country is more open and the great clean-floored beechwoods are not to be found except at Ashridge. But the Gaddesdens are in Chiltern country, as is Aldbury, with the Pendley Chapel in its church, a village green and a duckless duck pond. Here also are important sections of the mysterious Grimsditch which we shall be considering in some detail later. Berkhamsted and Tring are Chiltern towns, but there is only the castle site in the one, and the nature reserve made out of reservoirs feeding the Grand Union Canal in the other, to delay the tourist. But Graham Greene in his autobiography, *A Sort of Life*, feels that everything he has become and all he has written stems ultimately from Berkhamsted. There could scarcely be a higher commendation. On the extreme limit of the territory is Studham, worth a visit for the Norman font in the hideous cement-rendered church.

In the middle of Dunstable, indistinguishable now, as far as the motorist is concerned, from Luton, the age-old Icknield Way separates into its Upper and Lower parts for its journey through the Chilterns to Watlington. Behind Dunstable are the steep chalk downs on which 60 years ago the children tobogganed down the summer grass on tea trays and, in winter, the early skiers practised for Switzerland on a few inches of wet snow.

We have now defined the area in which we mean to work and write. In the course of this book we shall have journeyed from Studham to Reading, and from Slough to Thame and Long Crendon. We shall have walked on some of the ridges, motored on many deserted secondary roads, considered a few great houses and numerous churches. We shall have looked at some Chiltern oddities, remembered a few Chiltern worthies, pondered solutions to the two great Chiltern mysteries of the Grimsditch and the Icknield Way. We shall have glanced at the industries and suggested a number of pleasant motor and walking routes. Now and then we shall pause to think for a moment about the problems of today which have posed themselves in the age-old setting of these hills. This writer will not again intrude upon his reader. His only object in this book is that of a famous rock climber, the late Doctor Menlove Edwards, who, in his climbing guides to certain British rock faces, sought always 'to give the reader a general idea of the cliff before ever he comes to it'.

CHAPTER TWO

Some Chiltern
Churches

For centuries the parish churches of England, and in particular
the country churches, have been a focal point for almost every
communal activity and, since the church is invariably the first
building which any tourist wishes to see at any new point on his
route, it seems appropriate to devote an early chapter to considering the Chiltern churches as they are today. In some places they
are engulfed in a tide of new building and development, in others
they are much as they were at the Reformation. There are hundreds of them; the little map in Pevsner's *Buildings of Buckinghamshire*, to take only that one county, is almost black with dots,
most of them representing village churches; and so, in a general
book of this kind, it is only possible to take a few of the most
interesting or more beautifully situated, as representative of the
whole. There will naturally be many references to churches not
specifically mentioned in this chapter as the work proceeds as
nearly every tiny group of houses on the Chiltern maps, let
alone every small town and village, has a church of its own. It will
almost certainly date from mediaeval times, will probably be
mainly constructed, as to the exterior, of flint and brick, and in
most cases will be standing on the site of an earlier foundation. At
some time in the last hundred years or so the church, wherever it
is, will have been restored by loving but frequently ruthless hands,
but there will nearly always be something left to link its present
existence with the past; a font, a painting, an arrangement of oak

roofing beams, a tower or spire, a screen. Nearly always there will be a pamphlet or booklet just inside the door making a brave effort to link the past with the emptiness of the present. For the churches in the Chilterns will nearly always be empty, the remoter ones locked against possible vandalism, or because there is no longer a resident vicar or rector to keep an eye on things. From a strictly worldly point of view, there are now far too many churches in the Chilterns for the numbers wishing to use them or even, it would sometimes appear, to look at them. There are happy exceptions, of course. In the summer the church on the hill above West Wycombe will be crowded all day long, and there will always be someone in the church at Ewelme to see the stately loveliness of the first Duchess of Suffolk above her tomb, or the beauty of the shields on Thomas Chaucer's, or the soaring magnificence of the font cover. Someone is nearly always rubbing one or other of the famous brasses in Chinnor church, or looking at the murals in Little Kimble where the whole church has been declared a National Monument. In the main, however, the visitor will have most of the Chiltern churches entirely to himself, regardless of the time of year or of weather conditions.

Ewelme church is a must. Beautiful in itself it stands in an almost perfect English village, and there is a Ewelme Society to make sure that everything is preserved, as well and as naturally as possible, in an expanding community. Not long ago there was a proposal to take the new Benson/Watlington road either through or under the village, but this disaster was averted through the efforts of Miss Margaret Ritchie and the Ewelme Society. The church, the quiet English village in which it stands, the almshouses, and the oldest, entirely free, Church of England school in the country can all be enjoyed in their centuries-old natural surroundings of rural tranquility.

As it stands now the Church of St. Mary has been in Ewelme for 500 years, but there was a much earlier foundation, of All Saints. It was in that earlier church that Alice Chaucer, daughter of Thomas, and granddaughter of the poet Geoffrey, was married to William de la Pole, the first Duke of Suffolk. There is no marked period difference between the existing western tower, which formed a part of the earlier building, and the rest of the fabric. The Suffolk marriage took place in 1430 and it is almost certain that the present church was complete before the murder of the bridegroom 20 years later.

The amateur historian, or herald, will find days of interest stemming from this church. The armorial bearings on the Chaucer tomb, so splendidly and vividly restored, have all been worked out, and the results displayed for the benefit of visitors. The position of the Garter on the wrist of the Duchess of Suffolk's effigy was accepted by Queen Victoria and, later, also by Queen Mary as positive evidence of how the Garter should be worn by Ladies of the Order.

The chapel of St. John the Baptist in the church dates from 1437 when a Royal Licence was granted for the founding of the hospital, the Ewelme Almshouses. These form the oldest brick structure in the Chilterns and it has been suggested that the builders, working in such unfamiliar material, to any local craftsmen, must have come from the Suffolk estates in East Anglia, at Wingfield. The surname, Wingfield, is still to be found in the village. The almshouses, whose foundation document provides for 'two chaplains and thirteen poor men', draw their endowments from land in Ewelme, Marsh Gibbon (Bucks), Ramridge (Hants), and Conock (Wilts). Men from these parishes still have priority when appointments are made. The request of the Founders that the almsmen should be prayed for every day is still honoured, as is the principal rule of the adjoining Foundation school, the giving of an education to the children of Ewelme, 'Freely without any exaction of schole hire'. The outside of this school remains beautiful and unchanged, but the teaching methods employed are abreast or even ahead of contemporary educational thought.

Everything about the harmonious group of buildings in Ewelme, church, school and almshouses is of the greatest interest. In the church in addition to the world-famous font-cover, and the Suffolk and Chaucer monuments, there is much fine glass and some interesting brasses. There is also the mystery of the De la Pole grave.

There is an uninscribed blue stone in the church marking what is said to be the burial place of Michael de la Pole, who was killed at the Battle of Agincourt in 1415 and brought to Ewelme in a barrel of oil. It seems more likely that the claim of Burley Priory in Suffolk to possess the authentic tomb is correct; after all it is to Wingfield that one goes to see the de la Pole tombs in all their glory. It is perhaps worth mentioning as a comment on the general fate of armoured knights in mediaeval warfare that Michael de la Pole was one of only two noble casualties at Agincourt, the other being the Duke of York.

It is not easy to come away from Ewelme, so perfect and yet quietly changing with the times. There is a scattering of new buildings among the old, including a fine architect's studio. There is a flourishing watercress industry and over everything a sense of continuous history from Saxon beginnings. There is, finally, an interesting link in the church itself with the plainer church of similar age in Chinnor. The splendid roof of the church at Ewelme is new, dating from 1949-50. The main timbers came from Chinnor, which possesses the sixth oldest rood-screen in England, also made from local oak.

Within ten miles of Ewelme are two churches, St. Mary's at Turville, and St. Bartholemew's at Fingest, both worth a visit. The church at Turville is very old indeed, most of it certainly not later than 1100. This is a part of England where the Saxons held out longest against the Normans, the whole countryside being wild and inhospitable. For hundreds of years after the Conquest the neighbourhood of Turville provided a refuge for runaway serfs and outlaws, continuing to do so right up to the time of the highwaymen who rode out from Fingest to hold up the coaches making for Oxford. A quiet slow place, still.

At one time there was certainly a tower on St. Mary's church which is reputed to have fallen at some date prior to 1582. The plans for a new tower were drawn up in the reign of Mary Tudor and a beginning made, but nothing more was done beyond the buttresses still to be seen. The church was nearly lost in 1860 when the Parochial Church Council, taking a vocal line which at this writing is again being heard in some quarters, passed a resolution that the whole place be allowed to fall down, that the churchyard be closed, and the vicarage sold. The council wanted to build a new church in the then fashionable Gothic style, with a new vicarage to match, both being much nearer to the centre of the village. All this was vetoed by the Patron of the living and the Diocesan authorities, but they do not seem to have interfered in the restorations of 1875 during which great and irreparable harm was done to the church. The main problem faced by the restorers was that of certain foundations, rotted by centuries of burials close to the church walls and subsequent 'earthings up'. This was solved by pouring three feet of concrete over the sunken chancel to bring it up to the main floor level. In the process two sixteenth-century tombs were buried, and much mediaeval tiling. Additionally, the fourteenth-century piscina was rendered useless and the whole balance of the chancel arch destroyed. All the existing church furniture vanished at this time, together with the three-decker pulpit, thrown out or destroyed. There is much fine glass in the church, some of it modern, and there is the famous 'Blotted Escutcheon'. One of the windows commemorates the marriage of Humphrey Clarke and Mary Markham. Clarke died in the early part of the seventeenth century and, for a reason which has never been ascertained, Mary's surname was then blotted from the window. The last Vicar of Turville (the church is now administered as a member of the Hambleden Valley Group), found much ancient glass set into the vicarage door. He restored it to the church.

Only a mile or two away is the church of St. Bartholomew at Fingest. The main interest is the 800-year-old bifurcated tower, full of fourteenth-century oak. The restorers here were as dangerous and destructive in 1860 as, 15 years later, they were at Turville. They removed an eighteenth-century altar-piece together with the altar rails, and laid tiles throughout the church, including all over the east wall. Everything that could be done to put things right was begun in 1967, the church then (as with St. Mary's at Turville), being in the Hambleden Valley Group. Twenty years before that Sir John Betjeman in his *Murray's Guide to Bucking-hamshire* had written: 'inside the church has been swept and garnished and has little of interest to show'. Things are better now, but perhaps the time has come to give a little less prominence at the church gate, and in the historical brochure on sale within the church, to the somewhat over-written praises of the late Sir William Connor, 'Cassandra' of the *Daily Mirror*.

The church of St. Mary the Virgin, Hambleden, stands more or less as the fourth wall of one of the most beautiful and delightful Buckinghamshire villages. Some visitors will experience a sense of disappointment as they enter the church, it is so old and yet so shining, spotless and empty. But there was a church here 250 years before the Norman Conquest, wicked King John was Patron of the living in 1215 and King Charles II in 1666. There is a charming extract from one of the old registers to be seen on display in the church:

1680. The widow Chippes buried in Turvil who was the wife of six husbands, viz: Day, Strong, Tyler, Cool, Lever and Chippes.

Happy Mrs. Chippes to have had seven surnames in one lifetime and to be buried in Turville. But there is no record of her maiden name.

West Wycombe church stands 600 feet above the junction of the A40 London/Oxford road with the secondary road at the end of the village running over Bledlow Ridge. It is possible to drive a motor-car right up to the grass plateau at the side of the church, but it is more rewarding to walk up the face of the hill, the fine views, over an exceptionally wide arc, gradually unfolding.

As much nonsense has been written, talked and believed about this church as of any place in the whole of England. It has been suggested that even the site was chosen from sinister motives, and that the fine building with its great golden ball on the tower, dominating the country for miles around, was actually put there for 'the old oriental worship of Kybele, Rhea and Aphrodite'.

It may well be true that the rakes and bucks of the district called, with their friends from further afield, The Merry Monks of Medmenham, or, as they were sometimes called The Order of St. Francis of Wycombe and much later (long after most of them were dead and any survivors had become quiet-living elderly men), the Hell Fire Club, went in for a deal of hard drinking and debauchery. It may be true that John Wilkes did actually say that the interior of the golden ball, now closed to the public, was 'the best Globe Tavern I ever drank in', and it may even be true that a certain amount of loose behaviour went on in the caves below the church, always given that the ladies of that distant time could endure, after their long and dangerous journey from London, the bitter, unlighted, cold and all pervading damp of the galleries and chambers from which the metalled surface of the Wycombe road had been quarried. But none of that is evidence of devil worship in a church.

The Sir Francis Dashwood, who disported himself with Bubb Doddington and Wilkes, was later that English Chancellor of the Exchequer (under Lord Bute), who became the first Lord le Despenser, who made a version of the Prayer Book still much used in the United States today, and who rebuilt the church as it stands at present. That is hardly the sort of man, however wild his youth, who sets about the building of a nominally Christian church for the actual worship of evil.

Much has been made of the curious armchair lecterns in the church, so well fitted, it has been said, for the carrying out of 'strange rites'. But they must have come originally from some Italian monastery (the whole church is decorated in the Italianate style of the middle eighteenth century), and the contemporary monogram let into both of them, 'IHS' (JESUS the Salvation of Men) should alone be enough to dispel the legend of their suggested wicked purpose. Still wilder notions cling about the font, an Italian baroque artifact of the seventeenth century. Doves perch on it, a snake winds about it, the basin is less than a foot across. It is the kind of object which may well have been placed in or near the church quite casually; it can be lifted in one hand,

and it is not used for ordinary baptism except for members of the Dashwood family.

Any legend, once established, feeds and grows on repetition. It has been suggested that the dove symbol of the Holy Spirit in the chancel roof is 'a semi-philosophical development of the Medmenham hedonism'. It may be so; the box seats round the walls of the church may have been put there merely to hold the drink and habiliments of revelry, the golden ball set up as a drinking den. It is, however, a matter of fact that the church and everything in it was put there by a very rich man pleasantly indulging himself in the decorative tastes of the Enlightenment. And if indeed he rebuilt West Wycombe church as some reparation for youthful wildness, he was not the first man in history to do that.

There is a great deal to be seen and enjoyed in the Church of St. Andrew in Chinnor, far more than is generally recognised. The church, one of the largest in Oxfordshire, is not particularly inviting from outside and the more popular writers have usually dismissed it in a few lines as being very much a part of one of the ugliest, most scattered, and overbuilt villages in all the Chilterns. But it is well worth a visit. The plain rood screen made from locally-grown oak is more than 700 years old and still has its original wrought-iron hinges. The brasses are famous. They were removed from the floors in 1866 and, much later, put on the chancel wall as at present. Sir Reynald de Malyns, the knight in his armour, flanked by his two wives, is a grand sight. He was a Henton man, as Chinnor people would still say, and a member of a very powerful mediaeval family. The brasses of his wives have been much visited by historians of costume. Close by, on the same wall, is a very great treasure, called by Massingham 'one of the loveliest things to be seen in all the Chilterns', a foliated cross with the head of a priest at its centre. This commemorates William of Leicester who was Rector of Chinnor in 1314, and who rebuilt the chancel.

Only one mediaeval monument survives, the stone effigy of a knight, crossed legged and clad in armour. The legs are not crossed at the ankles, as they would be if the unknown knight had been on a Crusade, but are in the position called 'disturbed' or 'restless'. This may indicate that the knight had either taken oath for the Holy Land or had died when about to set out to join a Crusade. The monument is worn smooth and has been provisionally dated at around 1270.

There is some remarkable old glass in the church, notably in the north and south windows of the chancel. There is mediaeval glass in the east window also, but here it is mixed with nineteenth-century glass put in by the restorers. The pictures in the church, all reputed to be by Sir James Thornhill, the eighteenth-century painter, and to have come from St. Paul's Cathedral, were hung at the time of the 1866 restorations. At the back of the church and easily missed on a casual inspection hangs a contemporary coat of arms of Charles II, a somewhat rare occurrence in English churches.

The Chinnor bells are of major interest, spanning as they do the reigns of Elizabeth I, James I, and King Charles I and II. There are seven bells in all, retuned and rehung in 1969-70 as the result of a great and sustained local effort, the two smallest having been recast in 1864 from a tenor bell of 1651. The seventh bell is the first Churchill Bell in England, dedicated in 1965. The full peal is now to be heard ringing on all Sundays and major Feast days.

The font at the top of the north aisle should not be missed. It is a fourteeth-century, lead-lined piece of Purbeck marble, thrown out by the restorers and recovered from the churchyard in 1938 by Mr. William Clarke and Mr. Jack Caple at the instigation and expense of Mr. A. J. Manchester. There is much else of interest in and about the church, but perhaps enough has been said to indicate that had St. Andrew's Church had the good fortune to have remained in an unmolested setting it would have rated pages of guide-book eulogy. It is still a good place in which to rest, and pray.

Finally to Little Kimble. The church here, of All Saints, is very old, the Norman font being the original installation. It is however largely because of the fourteenth-century murals, now awaiting restoration, that the building has been scheduled as a National

Monument. It is still possible to identify St. Francis preaching to the birds, oddly enough one of only two pre-Reformation examples of this familiar subject to be found in the whole of England. There is a splendid representation of St. George, and St. Bernard can just be recognised with the help of the explanatory booklet to be found in the church. The other eight paintings must, at the moment, be taken largely on trust. Soon, when Mrs. Eve Baker begins what will undoubtedly be a major work of restoration, the walls will again be decorated as the original and unknown painter left them.

The church is tiny but has every desirable English feature. There is a grass path leading to it from the lych gate, double-banked with yews to lend a proper air of Byronic gloom. Not far away is Cymbeline's Castle, and the Icknield Way (here disguised as the London/Aylesbury road) runs past the gate. The land of Chequers, the Prime Minister's official country home marches with the church boundary. Ellesborough Church, and one of the great Chiltern views, is only a stroll away. The effort should be made.

6 *The Friends' Meeting House at Jordans. In the foreground*
the Penn and Ellwood graves
7 *The chancel and screen at Ellesborough, a 'lofted' or*
'moulded' Chiltern church

8 South front of *Ashridge House*

9 'Milton's Cottage', Chalfont St. Giles

Three Days in the Chilterns

There are nearly 3,000 miles of footpaths in the Chilterns, but nowadays the hard walker and the rambler tend to go farther afield and into wilder country. It is from a motor-car that most people will take, at any rate, their first look at the Chilterns and, with that in mind, the next few pages outline a motor tour which can be done comfortably in three days, which covers the whole area, and provides for reasonable pauses where there are matters of great interest to be discussed. To overcome too much repetition in later chapters, it will be found that an occasional dissertation or brief aside of a complementary nature is included.

The motorist should have with him Sheet 159 of the Inch-to-a-mile Ordnance Survey and, for close road directions, *Chiltern Country by Car*, a compilation by Peter and Helen Titchmarsh (White Horse Books, Stratford-on-Avon), which gives exact directions and mileages, taking always the quietest and most interesting roads, for a complete circular tour of all the Chilterns. There are numerous simple guide-books which are helpful, but for those with a deeper interest in the churches and buildings of the Chilterns than this book can hope to satisfy, there are the books by Sir Niklaus Pevsner or Sir John Betjeman. These are exhaustive.

It will be convenient to take the Buckinghamshire and Hertfordshire Chilterns first and to begin our own tour from Beaconsfield, with a visit to Jordans to look at the Quaker Settlement there. This, although less than two miles from Beaconsfield, and less than a mile from the A40 London/Oxford road, is deep in quiet Chiltern country. The Society of Friends maintains a meeting house here, dating from 1688, a hostel and guest house, and the Mayflower Barn, used mostly for concerts and similar gatherings. Everything is restful and beautiful, not least the carefully restored and maintained meeting house itself which, surprisingly, is big enough inside for 200 worshippers, if ever that number came. But it is the 11 simple gravestones on the lawn outside which draw the American tourists by hundreds every summer. They mark the resting places of William Penn and his two wives, his two daughters Letitia and Aubrey Margaret Froame, and the five of his children who died in infancy. His sons Springett and John are there, and behind are the graves of Thomas Ellwood and his wife Mary. It is not strictly in accordance with Quaker traditions that these graves are marked at all, and the stones date only from 1862 or thereabouts. But nearly always in the summer there is someone, or a small party, standing reverently by these graves and, if they are Americans, they will be thinking about the Founder of Pennsylvania, that State where, 'white man and Indian should live in amity, and freedom of conscience be respected'. There are now scores of other graves (with the same simple rounded headstones) at the back of the lawn, but they are as unremarkable as those who lie in them would wish.

For British visitors the graves of Mary and Thomas Ellwood have a special interest, but the natural place to think and write about Thomas is in the Chalfonts, at the so called 'Milton's Cottage' which belonged to him. Before leaving Jordans, however, the Mayflower Barn should be visited. This is almost certainly largely constructed from the timbers of the famous Pilgrim ship after she had been broken up at Harwich in 1624. The farmhouse (now the hostel) is of the same date as the barn and main beams in both house and barn were certainly taken from a ship. One of the beams in the barn is cracked across and repaired in exactly the manner recorded of a mishap in the *Mayflower* on her Pilgrim voyage. There is a door in the hostel (which incidentally was used as a Quaker meeting house before the building of the present one) which might well have been a cabin door. It has a mayflower carved upon it.

It is a short run from Jordans to the Chalfonts, and the cottage which Thomas Ellwood lent to Milton at the time of the Great Plague. There are legends that Milton finished *Paradise Lost* in this cottage and that, at Ellwood's insistence he began to write *Paradise Regained*. There is, however, no evidence that he did any work at all during his comparatively short stay. Ellwood had been his Latin tutor and was always his friend.

Ellwood thought of himself as a poet and, after he became a Quaker, suffered grievously for his faith, being imprisoned at one time or another in London, High Wycombe and Aylesbury. His cottage ought to be visited; it is kept strictly and neatly as in Milton's time, but there is nothing else in the Chalfonts to delay the motorist.

The scene, of endless streets and houses, changes with startling abruptness three miles from Little Chalfont, at Chenies. In the church here the Dukes of Bedford lie buried in their own chapel, separated from the main body of the church by a great glass screen. There are difficulties about obtaining entry to the Bedford Chapel, but the beauty and excitement of the monuments, and there is nothing like them elsewhere in England, is vividly experienced from the church side of the screen. The church itself, basically a fifteenth-century building, is much restored.

Only a mile or so away is the village of Latimer, its cottages set about a small green. The manor house close by the village is now a Staff College and there is much land about it taken up by service hutments. But the River Chess is here, and typical Chiltern woodlands everywhere around. The drive out of the village, towards Berkhamsted, is particularly beautiful.

Berkhamsted is a Chiltern town which has lost all its character. The castle remains are scarcely more than a pleasant open space and there is little else to detain the tourist. Drive on instead, remaining in open country, towards Wigginton and the high Chiltern crossing of the Grand Union Canal at Cow Roast Inn. This route crosses the Chesham/Berkhamsted road at Ashley Green, but modern taste will find little in the Victorian Gothic church of St. John there to make a visit to it rewarding. From Wigginton there is one of the great Chiltern views, and only two miles or so away, and almost part of Berkhamsted at Northchurch, is a building said to be the oldest Christian church in the world. All about is much of peculiarly Chiltern interest, stretches of the Grimsditch, patches of heath and woodland, and the like. But our main business must be at Cow Roast, and the canal at over 600 feet on its climb out of London through Gerrards Cross. Between Cow Roast and Berkhamsted there are 17 locks in just over seven miles, all on what was originally the Grand Junction Canal, cut with pick and shovel between 1793 and 1806, 13 years of perhaps the hardest hand labour in the world. The whole Grand Union system was only formed in 1929, passing to the British Transport Commission in 1948, and to the British Waterways Board in 1963.

The Canal is crossed twice between Cow Roast and Aldbury, a most beautiful village with everything a visitor, and especially an overseas visitor, expects to find in the English countryside. There is still a horsepond; all the cottages have been there for centuries; the old stocks have been preserved. The church here must not be missed, if only for the Pendley Chapel with its superb Perpendicular screen around the tomb of Sir Richard Whittinhame and his wife.

It is worth branching off the road between Aldbury and Little Gaddesden to climb the Bridgewater Monument, a memorial to the third Duke who pioneered so much of the canal system we have just left. There is a small charge for admission to the Monument, but the views are worth it. Back then to Little Gaddesden, and the 4,000 acres of National Trust forest on the Ashridge Estates. At all times of the year these rich woodlands will have cars parked thickly along the verges, but there are endless trails and pathways into and through the woods and a short walk anywhere is a delightful experience. In the village itself are many beautiful cottages, some of them skilful enlargements and restorations from the days when foresters and gamekeepers and other workers lived in them in the time of private ownership here, but the main objective should be the church, well away from the village and standing at the end of a semi-private road. Here are Bridgewater monuments in great profusion, perhaps a trifle oppressive for modern tastes, but recalling persons of immense importance in the history of England. Perhaps the greatest attraction of this church is the marvellous view eastwards from the back of it. This is truly one of the great English views and on a clear sunny day provides an experience which the fortunate visitor will never forget.

It is hardly worth-while to push out to the extremity of the Hertfordshire Chilterns at Studham, where there is an ugly cement-rendered church of great age with a Norman font. At Little Gaddesden we are close to national rather than especially Chiltern places of interest, the zoo at Whipsnade, Ivinghoe Beacon (an Iron Age hill fort), and the oldest actually dated windmill (1627) in England at Pitstone. There is also the artificial, but none the worse for that, Tree Cathedral, near Tring: this is now National Trust property. Our second day will take us through some of the best of the Buckinghamshire Chilterns and into some of the wilder areas beneath the Oxfordshire ridge.

Wendover, although not on the direct route, is almost exactly half-way between Aylesbury and Tring. This is the town Robert Louis Stevenson called 'a straggling purposeless sort of place', an opinion endorsed by Massingham half a century later. But it is very much a Chiltern town, and has more to it than that description would imply. The Upper Icknield Way runs through it and the Lower Way is not far off. There is a stretch of the Grimsditch within half a mile, and there is Coombe Hill beyond the town with a Boer War memorial at nearly 800 feet, and splendid views over the Vale of Aylesbury, and in the direction of the Cotswolds. It is said that on a clear day St. Paul's can be seen, 38 miles away. It was probably from here that William Cobbett made his famous remark, looking out over the Vale, that so beautiful a country would never have to suffer unworthy rulers. The church at Wendover (St. Mary's) should not be missed. It is a much-restored building and the outside has no attraction for the motorist, but inside is the moving brass plate (1537) to William Bradshawe and his wife. There they are with, below them, their nine children kneeling in a row, and, beneath them again, the names of their 23 grandchildren. Wendover has grown rapidly in recent years but it is still a restful place with a true country town atmosphere.

Within the triangle Wendover, Great Missenden, Princes Risborough, lies almost the best of the Buckinghamshire Chilterns. Here are to be found Great and Little Hampden, Great and Little Kimble, Chequers, Ellesborough, with another Chiltern view from Cymbeline's Mount, or from the door of Ellesborough Church itself. Here also is Lacey Green, and Speen, with the beautifully named Pink and Lily public house, immortalised by Rupert Brooke in a piece of light-hearted doggerel, Whiteleaf Cross, a long stretch of Grimsditch and, mile after mile of traffic-free, tree-bordered secondary and tertiary roads. At a later stage some of these places and matters will be considered at greater length. There is so much to see and enjoy, for instance the church at Great Hampden with the memorials and relics of the man who refused to pay Ship Money, and was mortally wounded in the first real battle (Chalgrove Field) of the Civil War which grew out of that imposition. Hampden's house is now a school and is not shown except by special arrangement.

There are several routes which might be taken between Wendover and Princes Risborough, but the longest is the best. It is really worth-while to cast back to Great Missenden and to wind all the way from there to the main Wendover/Princes Risborough road at Monks Risborough. This is all wooded hill country and conveys much of the magnetic attraction this part of the world has for a whole new population.

Princes Risborough, now a part of High Wycombe Rural District, has nothing much for the tourist but is still a charming Buckinghamshire small town with, as usual nowadays in all this part of the world, considerable outlying 'developments'. It is true that there is now a small supermarket in Princes Risborough, but a recent description of the town as, 'struggling against the supermarket age', is very wide of the mark. The whole wide-street area (it is in no sense a 'square') which holds the church, a late seventeenth-century manor house (National Trust), the market house, and a group of old shops is almost exactly as it was 40 years ago. Some of the names on the shops and the houses of business men have changed, but not the branch of the County Library in a lovely pair of old cottages, heavily timbered. No one standing in Princes Risborough could or need feel that all is lost. Sir John Betjeman, writing in the 1948 *Murray's Guide to Buckinghamshire* on which he collaborated with the painter John Piper, had some unkind things to say about the place, a first impression of 'untidy Metroland below the Chilterns', a Roman Catholic Church, 'jazz modern and anxious to be different', but the little town has stood up well in the quarter century since then.

Between three and four miles from Princes Risborough is the overgrown village of Chinnor, our entry to the Oxfordshire Chilterns. Those who do not know the village tend to speak of it as 'that place with a cement works', but it is more than that. The Romans were here, working the chalk for their lime mortar and concrete. The Saxons had a church here on the site of the present St. Andrew's church, itself a fourteenth-century foundation. It is not true that 'Chinnor is perpetually powdered with cement dust', but it *is* true that the village has been strained far beyond its capacity to absorb people. Yet a further building scheme is envisaged, and it seems probable that Chinnor is being deliberately 'let go' in order to save many surrounding villages. In the long run this decision from Whitehall, overruling both the Parish and County Councils, may prove to have been correct, but the deliberate creation of almost slum conditions in parts of the village, with an educational problem of frightening dimensions less than five years away, is hard for the existing residents to accept.

Yet all around Chinnor is one of the most beautiful and unspoilt countrysides in England. Only two miles away is Bledlow, with its persisting legend that William the Conqueror was actually there in person, and with an ancient church rebuilt on one of the earliest Norman foundations. This is the church, by a tiny stream, the Lyde, about which an old saying has it, 'They that live and do abide shall see Bledlow Church fall into the Lyde'. But too many of these pleasant diversions, to the charming little church at Radnage for example, cannot be made on a definite tour and from Chinnor the Watlington road should be taken. This runs through Aston Rowant and across the A40 to Lewknor, a village to be split, it is said, by the new M4 extensions. A route for this motorway has been proposed which would save Lewknor, together with the only completely unspoiled Chiltern ridge. This is the much publicised Arup-Jellicoe Route which has been supported by every amenity society in the Chilterns; but it was devised somewhat late in the day and has been rejected by the road planning departments in Whitehall.

By English standards nearly all the scenery between Chinnor and Watlington is new; very little of it is earlier than 1830 and the virtual completion of enclosures under the various Settlement and Parliament Acts. It is a pleasant road and it leads to a delightful place. Watlington is quite unspoiled and, with the branch line to Princes Risborough closed and itself somewhat 'off the map' it is likely to remain so. Above the town lies Christmas Common and Watlington Hill and the climb, by motor-car (turning sharp left exactly as the little town is entered from the Chinnor direction) should be made. The views from the top are staggering and, being under the National Trust, the whole summit area is open to the public. The obelisk cut into the chalk is probably eighteenth century, although attempts have been made to demonstrate that it is a megalithic sun pointer.

There is now, for those adhering to the circular tour, a choice of route, through Britwell Salome and Ewelme to Ipsden, Goring, Mapledurham and the river towns, or through the heart of the Oxfordshire Chilterns, reserving until later a casting back from Henley-on-Thames (where the second night might well be spent) to reverse the Goring, Watlington route. This last is preferable if the Chilterns are new to the wayfarer. From Christmas Common then we take, on B roads all the way, the road to Turville, Fingest and Hambleden. This whole run is in classic Chiltern country, every side-turning leading deep into woodlands, the names on the map enchanting. We have already looked at the churches in Fingest and Turville and here our concern is with those villages themselves. Both are lovely and, on the right day, magical. Beyond is Skirmett and Skirmett wood which Massingham feared, so recently as 1940, might altogether disappear. It is still much as he saw it, and indeed in all this area you will find nothing but wooded English countryside with no suggestion anywhere of over-crowded unplanned development, or wanton destruction. At Pheasants Hill there is a view over all the Hambleden Valley, preparing the motorist for Hambleden village and the old white-fronted watermill. From here it is only a short run to Henley-on-Thames.

The river towns of the Chilterns can be left for another occasion. On this journey we cast back, now, through a fresh section of the deep Oxfordshire Chilterns, towards Ewelme. The best route for scenery and interest is by B roads through Rotherfield Greys and on to Rotherfield Peppard in order to come up through steep wooded lanes to Checkendon and Nuffield. Ewelme is then only two or three miles away. By taking this route we shall see something of the Chiltern heaths, or perhaps, rather, something of what is now left of them. These were once as characteristic of the area, in certain parts of the Chilterns, as the beechwoods themselves. But now Reading has grown out to influence all the surrounding country, and much new building has swamped these heathlands. No matter, we have seen, in approaching them, some of the best of the superb Chiltern sameness, and we shall have paused at Checkendon church. If the Chilterns have two hearts then this is one of them, the other being all the country around Stonor and Fawley. But in that connection some say that there is nothing anywhere to compare with the deep peace of Wormsley, just a mile from the A40, where the deer will come out of the woods to look curiously at the stranger.

Massingham thought Checkendon church the best in all the south, except Ewelme and the tower of the church at Fingest. The murals there are beautiful and much else has escaped the restorer's hand. Massingham wrote that he longed to take William Cobbett to Checkendon; but that would have been a wasted journey indeed. Cobbett's indignation about great churches too large for their villages has no relevance to present-day situations. Cobbett thought the big churches would actually draw towns towards them. The towns have come, but the big churches (and the small), stand empty.

There is, as we already know from our visit to the church, nothing in the Chilterns to compare with Ewelme. Barely inside the area at all, it is yet the queen of it. Full of light and colour, in an atmosphere of peace and contentment, Ewelme may be the only place left in England where the school, the almshouses and the work of the Church are all being conducted in exactly the manner the founders intended on the sites where they built. There is nothing better for 50 miles in any direction.

Between three and four miles from Ewelme, on the Goring side of the A4130, there is a characteristic stretch of the Grimsditch which invites a pause to consider this 'longest serpent of antiquity'. The surrounding countryside is about to become open and unforested, but here all is as it should be and the spot is ideal for leaving the car and walking for a few hundred yards along the thickly hedgerowed dyke. There are so many points of view about the nature of the Grimsditch and its purpose that it would be confusing to cite them here. The ditch sprawls across the Chiltern map, sometimes as just a few hundred yards of old earthwork, sometimes, when between Bradenham and Ashridge, as more than 15 miles of clearly defined barrier. The ramp of the ditch is everywhere taller than a man, even now, hundreds of years after the first constructions. Here and there it is as much as 40 feet high, with a fosse 30 feet deep. All the Chiltern writers have put forward their theories, but there is now more or less general agreement, in the absence of any proof, indeed in the much stranger absence of any legends or traditions, that the Grimsditch is all we have left of an ancient frontier between Mercia and Wessex. It is certainly no earlier than those late Saxon times.

Not far from this point on the Grimsditch there is a stretch of the Icknield Way, which might also be considered here. The Way is the ancient Green Road through England and is the oldest prehistoric track in the country, or perhaps in any country. Its main route is from East Anglia to Avebury in Wiltshire, but throughout the Chilterns, from the centre of Dunstable to Watlington the Way is split into Upper and Lower sections.

Much of the Way has been subjected to alteration and improvement over the centuries. The Romans found it and used it, even paved long sections of it. In some places the ruts of their chariot wheels can still be seen, and here and there edible Roman snails are still living and breeding beside the Way.

But the Green Road was thousands of years old before the Romans came to Britain. Bronze Age man must have known it, and helped to create parts of it, 2,000 years before the birth of Christ. It has been suggested that for many centuries there was no Upper Way as we know it; that the high route through the Chilterns was made by more or less random wanderings across dry open slopes to avoid the dark forests and the stiff clays of the valleys. This theory, of Mr. Annan Dickson's, makes sense. No two walkers ever take the same path across the lower slopes of a mountain, but over many years or even centuries a track often becomes defined along the simplest and most direct route. There was no need for the horsemen and early users of an Upper Way to 'stay on the footpath'; they would have picked their way. Everywhere in the Chilterns the Upper Way commands the scene and it was at such levels that our earliest pit-dwelling forefathers chose to live. There are several of their 'complexes' at different points along the Way, as there are of later generations of emerging western man.

All over the Chilterns the visitor will be coming across sections of the Icknield Way, both Upper and Lower. Sometimes he will find the Way as a careful upland preservation, sometimes as a main traffic artery. Perhaps Chinnor is the best headquarters for a serious study of the Way, the Upper and Lower reaches being less than a mile apart there and in both cases continuing as long clearly defined routes in open country.

We leave both the Way and the Grimsditch behind us and

motor through open rolling country, quite unlike any other part of the Chilterns, to Goring. On the route it is worth turning aside for a few hundred yards to look inside the church at Ipsden, if only to see the north aisle, in effect a large room, in which meetings can be and are held. No church like this is to be seen anywhere else.

All river towns, even in the Chilterns are much the same, delightful in the early part of the year and in the autumn, badly overcrowded in summertime. After leaving Goring we make our way across Chiltern heath country to Mapledurham, passing on the way Alnut's Hospital, an early eighteenth-century foundation of almshouses, school and chapel not open to the public but still (as at Ewelme) functioning as the Founder intended.

The great house at Mapledurham was almost in ruins until about 12 years ago when the owner, Mr. J. J. Eyston, a direct descendant of the original fifteenth-century builder of the house, Sir Michael Blount, set about the long task of restoration. The mill in a somewhat dilapidated state is still beautiful and it is said that one day Mr. Eyston intends to restore it also in its perfect setting. The church, which is all part of the scene, is usually locked, but the key is readily available nearby. Part of it is a Roman Catholic chapel. Mapledurham House itself is only shown at certain times of the year and then only on certain days. It is very much a superb private house.

Henley, like Goring, needs no description, particularly as for a week every year it is exposed on television during the international regatta. But, at the end of the Fairmile out of the town, the sign 'Watlington' leads the motorist once again into the loveliest Chiltern country, any side-turning he may care to take leading to fresh enchantments. One such turning runs into Fawley where the church should not be missed as a great surprise awaits the visitor. So truly English outside, the interior is almost pure eighteenth-century Italian.

From Fawley it is easy to reach Hambleden Mill, and the village of Hambleden, going on thence through Medmenham to Marlow. Medmenham is a quiet place now, but the deserted abbey here was once a meeting place for those Merry Monks whose legends we encountered around West Wycombe church. We go on through Marlow where there is a bridge (1832) by the same Clarke who built a similar but much greater crossing at Buda Pesth. The spire of the parish church at Marlow is by Scott, as is the spire at Princes Risborough, but the church itself is lacking in interest except for the coach-accident memorial in the porch.

From Marlow, and all in Chiltern country, we should visit Cookham (Stanley Spencer Gallery) and the famous Boulter's Lock, one of the great Sunday attractions in the summers of Edwardian England. Then on through Taplow, all the while close to the Thames, at last bending away for Cliveden and Burnham Beeches. Cliveden has been National Trust property for 30 years now, the beautifully laid out grounds and gardens rather than the house being the principal attraction.

Burnham Beeches is another of our Chiltern limits. It is all the property of the Corporation of the City of London and is well worth a week-day visit. The entire area is now densely populated but the great pollarded trees give an excellent idea of what the old Chiltern country must have been like, as indeed do Bockmer woods which we passed through between Medmenham and Marlow. The run into Beaconsfield from Burnham completes our Chiltern ring. But it would not do to leave out High Wycombe which occupies the very centre of the Chiltern map, and whose great furniture industry was originally based on the Chiltern beechwoods. On this last diversion we must travel another marvellous stretch of forgotten Chilterns, beginning at West Wycombe and running through Radnage to the summits of Chinnor and Crowell Hills. We should also visit Hughenden, to stand for a moment beside the Disraeli graves, going on to Penn, which is by no means the suburb of High Wycombe it has recently been called, but a Chiltern village in its own right well worth seeing.

We have now taken fleeting glances at practically all the Chiltern country and it is time to make specific pilgrimages to some of the places we have passed through or paused at all too briefly. We shall discuss some of the legends about them or look at the historical facts. We shall examine some of the industries which are in the Chilterns because of the nature of the country, and discourse here and there on matters which, essentially Chiltern in substance, are yet of general interest. There is much to see, and to discuss.

CHAPTER FOUR

The Chiltern Towns

Elderly Chiltern residents are perhaps over inclined nowadays to dwell in the past, and to think and speak as though the entire 500 square miles were under bricks and mortar, and the little Chiltern townships (for that is what they mostly are) rapidly expanding cities. Yet, leaving out Slough, which is a special case, High Wycombe with a population below 80,000 is the biggest place in the area. It is true that the whole southern escarpment, the right-hand line of the Chilterns as you open the map, is marred by overbuilding and over-development to a point beyond redemption as far as this generation can see; but although there is nothing to hold the tourist in Slough, Gerrards Cross, the Chalfonts, Chesham, or Berkhamsted there is perhaps something for the reader.

It was in 1786 that William Herschel, the astronomer, moved from Datchet to Slough in order to set up his great telescope in a place free from noise and vibration, in his garden there. Slough was then a sleepy market town with a population of 4,000 or 5,000, and it remained so until the war of 1914-18. Immediately afterwards a huge dump was formed outside Slough for the storage of supplies of now useless war material, and it was to get some order into the chaos which resulted in the Slough Trading Estate being formed as a development company. The main object after disposing of the surplus materials was to attract light industry in order to make use of the acres of store sheds and temporary offices on the site. The overpowering growth of the town and the adjacent Trading Estate is the measure of the success achieved. It is difficult, standing in the middle of present-day Slough, to realise that the perfect peace of Eton is just up the road and that it is not two miles to the 'country churchyard' of Stoke Poges, the scene of Gray's world famous Elegy. Pevsner says of Slough: 'It is a town without tradition; it did not become a Civil Parish until 1894 and has not made any efforts yet to build up any visual centre of dignity. It could have done, but has not.' This is not altogether fair; the map shews at a glance what has happened to Slough and there is not a town council in the country capable of handling an expansionist rush which took on some of the aspects of an avalanche. It is, perhaps, worth mentioning that Slough was almost the first place in England, if not the very first, to inaugurate road safety campaigns, to draw attention to the needs and anxieties of pedestrians, and to do something positive about the control of pets in the streets. Such matters, although not spectacular are of great importance in a motorised and pollution-conscious age.

There is probably not an English-speaking child in the world who has not heard or been compelled to learn by heart a few of those verses beginning 'The curfew tolls the knell of parting day'. It is sentiment, engendered by recollection of the immortal lines rather than what is actually there, which now impels the tourist to Stoke Poges. Only the dedicated sightseer will wish to do more than glance up at the 'ivy mantled tower' standing above the roar of the traffic, and perhaps spend a moment at the Gray memorial in the churchyard. In the Chilterns, as elsewhere, there is sometimes disappointment when a long-cherished image is seen in an atmosphere of harsh reality. It has recently been suggested that St. Peter's Church, Burnham was the real scene of the poet's inspiration.

There is an Iron Age fort, said to be the largest in England, near Bulstrode Park, at Gerrards Cross, but there is also the Church of St. James, built in 1869 as a memorial to Major-General Reid. This is more than worth a brief visit if only to enjoy the dome in the light of Pevsner's description of it, 'here the *Rundbogenstil* breaks down and the High Victorian is triumphant'. But this Italianate church represents the attempt of a Victorian architect,

10 *An unspoiled lane near Berkhamsted*

Sir William Tite, to break out of his imprisoning Gothic cage and, on the whole, he succeeded.

The Chalfonts are now completely obliterated, London suburbs with remnants of their Chiltern origins. There are a few patches of common, even an actual village green among the houses, but nearby Amersham has much of interest still. The Drake monuments in the Church of St. Mary are more numerous and noteworthy than those of any church in Buckinghamshire, except for those in the Bedford chapel at Chenies. The main street of the town is still exceptionally attractive, and only a mile away is the plain-fronted Drake mansion of Shardeloes, much of it by Robert Adam. For those who may forget the traditions of this area there is in Amersham an ultra-Protestant memorial of a kind unlikely to be found elsewhere. But it is the only monument anywhere in the Chilterns to remind us of the Chiltern men who were hanged or burned in St. Giles Fields, outside London, for their part in Sir John Oldcastle's rebellion. The memorial would have us believe that these men died for the Protestant religion (not then devised), but the point is immaterial. They died, nameless, for their Lollard principles and are here remembered.

Chesham has lost its Chiltern character entirely although the approaches to it, and to Chesham Bois, are characteristically steep and there are still many trees. But all about are brick wildernesses which continue to expand.

In so brief a review of Chiltern towns it is reasonable to leave out Berkhamsted and Tring altogether (there is nothing in the slightest degree 'Chiltern' about either) and to drive once more into Wendover, this time in order to make a decision about Aylesbury. We have already seen that everyone visiting Wendover goes into the church to look at the Bradshawe memorial brass and to think about the fates of little Alice and Brigid, and Sybell and Johan, dust for centuries; but from Coombe Hill, also previously visited, the Vale of Aylesbury can be seen in all its beauty, reminding us that even in a Chiltern book, the town of Aylesbury cannot be ignored. The whole line of the Buckingham-

11 *Whiteleaf Cross above Princes Risborough*

shire Chilterns overlooks the Vale, as do the Hertfordshire Chilterns from say Pitstone: nowhere in Chiltern country can the Vale be ignored or forgotten. Aylesbury itself is no longer a typical market and county town, but flourishes exceedingly, with much well-planned development and so elaborate a road system of approach and departure that the casual visitor finds entry difficult and departure well-nigh impossible. From the outskirts of the town the ridge view of the Chilterns is superb, principally because the original Aylesbury was planned and built on rising ground. It is strange that so old a town has so new a look. All the events of English history affected Aylesbury, many of them occurring in it or near it. But Aylesbury has always kept up with the times and there is no feeling anywhere not even inside the church, of the mediaeval town which in fact it is.

With Aylesbury, and with the exception of High Wycombe, we have finished with urban life in the Chilterns. There is Watlington, and, on the fringe of the territory, Thame. All the rest of this allegedly overbuilt and overcrowded Chiltern England is open or densely wooded country, villages, some of them expanding, most of them much the same as they were at the turn of the century, numerous hamlets, random groups of houses. Everyone enjoys coming across Watlington, but no one would go there to spend the day with sightseeing in mind. There is nothing better in England than Christmas Common and Watlington Hill above the town. *That* is where visitors to Watlington should go, and where they will be rewarded beyond their expectations.

There remains High Wycombe which if it were being considered in all its aspects would need a chapter to itself; as indeed would even the smallest town in the Chilterns if anything like a detailed history were to be attempted. The industries which have produced High Wycombe are based, or were originally based, on the woodlands all around, or on the fast-running miniature river, the Wye, which begins above the village of West Wycombe and ends its course in the Thames at Marlow. In the past it turned a number of paper mills during this short journey, notably at Loudwater. The mills, no longer water-powered, are still much in evidence and fully productive.

Furniture is the great High Wycombe industry and there are said to be 138 factories within the town making every kind of furniture for home and export. Later on something will have to be said about the forests and traditions of hand wood-turning which gradually drew these factories into one place, but the town itself, greatly expanded in recent years is of much interest. In the near future it will all be seen again as it originally was, the endless miles of the 'High Wycombe Bottleneck' forgotten. For the new by-passes and M4 extensions are either finished or nearing completion and already after many years it is again possible to stand and look at Keene's little Guildhall, and to park a motor-car before visiting the ancient and beautiful church. For the motorist or casual visitor it is not these things which are the special feature of High Wycombe but the Rye, a great open space of meadow land which belongs to the town and greets the visitor driving in from London as he enters the five-mile-long town squeezed between two Chiltern ridges. There is never any doubt in High Wycombe about actually being in the Chilterns. All the side streets are steeper than ordinary comfort would wish, and if the shopper lifts her head there are trees.

So much for the Chiltern towns. In the course of this book we shall be running in and out of many of them again. They have all changed greatly in recent years with perhaps the solitary exception of the closely guarded and preserved Watlington. But over the centuries all the little towns have profoundly affected their surrounding countrysides and thus in all of them the Chiltern atmosphere still makes itself felt.

CHAPTER FIVE

Some Anecdotes, Beliefs and Curiosities

The listing of Chiltern towns inevitably produces recollections about some of them, or anecdotes concerning them. Beaconsfield is such a place. When we first encountered it we were concerned mainly with Jordans and the Quaker Settlement, but there is much of great interest surviving in the town itself, particularly old Beaconsfield. There is now a purely dormitory settlement of new Beaconsfield, mainly for persons in comfortable circumstances, which is of no interest in a book of this kind.

Old Beaconsfield abuts on, or adjoins, the London/Oxford road. Burke, the great orator and essayist lived nearby and is commemorated in the church, as, in the churchyard, is Edmund Waller, the poet of 'Go lovely rose, tell her who wastes her time and me', and a true Beaconsfield man. Benjamin Disraeli took his title from here, but his first home was at Bradenham, not far from High Wycombe on the Princes Risborough road, where his father, Isaac, 'the king of all the bookworms', wore out his eyes producing his wonderful *Curiosities of Literature*.

In the hey-day of the rotten boroughs the Member of Parliament for Aylesbury, Mr. du Pré, lived at Wilton Park, Beaconsfield. At one election he forgot to bribe the electors—there were never very many of them, still less than 30 when the young Benjamin Disraeli first contested, and lost, the seat—and they invited him to a funeral. On arrival Mr. du Pré found it was a mock ceremony over his own 'remains' and that the mourners expected 'benevolences'. He was quick to take the point, at once distributed three guineas a head and was returned at the top of the poll the next time he put himself to the vote.

Beaconsfield was also a local headquarters of the notorious high-wayman Claude Duval whose sword cuts, made when resisting capture, are said still to be on the staircase at the George.

On the road between Beaconsfield and High Wycombe there is an easily missed Tithing Stone on the parish boundary, at Holtspur. It commemorates, or celebrates, a defeat for the Rector of Beacons-field in 1827. He had tried to get local practices altered in his favour, but opposition to custom is nearly always a lost cause in England. The stone reads, '3rd., May 1827. Boundary stone of the Manor and Parish of Beaconsfield. The custom of Tithing corn in this Parish is (and has been immemorially) by the Tenth Cock and the Eleventh Shock.' That is a splendid thing to read now, as there has not been a true tithe in England since 1936, when the last of these perpetual agricultural irritations was removed by Act of Parliament.

There is a little more to say about Wendover. Long before the Bradshawe brass was put into the church, Roger of Wendover was experiencing and writing about the starvation year of 1234 when in July 'the poor people who daily suffered from want rushed into the harvest fields in crowds and plucked the ears of corn although not yet ripe, and bruising them up with trembling hands, en-deavoured to sustain the spark of unhappy life which still pal-pitated in their bosoms'. It is difficult to believe this in the prosperous Wendover of today, motor-cars parked everywhere, well dressed men and women parading the streets. But man has always been barely a step away from starvation if the elements turn against him, as in the United States 'Dust bowl' of the 1920s or Pakistan in 1970. We can be more cheerful in the villages sur-rounding Wendover, Great Hampden for instance. As recently as 1950 it was possible for a Chiltern writer to begin a description of Great Hampden with the sentence, 'ranks with Stoke Poges in its union of country charms and personal associations'. Alas for Stoke Poges, but Great Hampden (it is not a true village but rather a collection of scattered houses) is still much as it always has been. Its association with 'Ship Money' Hampden will never be broken while our history is read, and he lies buried in the church, as we have already seen. But there is also Little Hampden on the road between Princes Risborough and Great Missenden where the murals in the church should not be missed. They were only discovered in 1907 and the picture of St. Christopher, thought to be not later than 1273, is the earliest reproduction of that now believed to be entirely legendary Saint in England. There is another early St. Christopher, probably fourteenth century, in the church at Little Missenden. This was uncovered in 1931 but was almost certainly painted at the time of the 'scenes from the life of St. Catharine' also on the walls. There are fishes playing about St. Christopher's feet.

The beginnings of the struggle between King and Parliament which led to our Civil War did not occur at either of the Hampdens or in John Hampden's house, but at Great Kimble. It was to the church here that Hampden, who owned the Manor of Kimball, came from his house, in January 1635, and refused to pay his assessment. The actual proceedings against him took place two years later, and were based on his similar refusal in the neighbouring parish of Stoke Mandeville, but it was in Great Kimble church that the first 'confrontation', as we should say nowadays, took place.

It is in the Kimbles that the Prime Ministers of England have had a country home since 1917 (or, as some have it, 1920), when Lord Lee of Fareham gave his great country house, Chequers Court, to the nation for that purpose. For obvious reasons the house is not open to the public, but it has been much altered and restored over the centuries since the original building of 1565. Most of the land of Chequers is in Ellesborough parish, with its Church-on-a-Hill by Cymbeline's Mount. It has already been suggested that this church be visited after seeing the murals in Little Kimble church, largely because it is here that Vale and Chilterns meet and the beauty of both may be experienced to the full.

It is at this point that Whiteleaf, and the landmark of Whiteleaf Cross, fall naturally to be discussed, and it will prove convenient to add a few notes on some other Chiltern curiosities, legends, beliefs, and those actual objects, such as the Cook memorial in Chalfont St. Giles, which draw visitors to a particular place.

The Cross at Whiteleaf is visible for miles in two directions, and is perhaps best seen either across the valley from Bledlow Ridge, or from the Thame or Chinnor roads as they approach Princes Risborough. This chalk cutting has at one time or another been given every date from prehistoric times until the middle of the eighteenth century when, in 1738, the Rev. Francis Wise made the first mention of the cross to be found in the literature. There is no reason to suppose that the cross, or pedestal with a rough cross upon it, has anything to do with the prehistory of our country. Indeed, if the carving was intended as a cross then Neolithic man can have had nothing to do with it. We should perhaps be satisfied with the 250 years of history we know about in connection with Whiteleaf which is now scheduled as a National Monument. If indeed it was there in earlier times and was carved in connection, as some hold, with the obelisk at Watlington, then it may well be that the monks of Whiteleaf (there was a monastery at Monks Risborough in the days before the Dissolutions) carved a crude armpiece to make a cross from the phallic sculpture near their home.

The Chilterns lend themselves to legends and speculations. For the whole of recorded time man has gone up into high places for prayer and meditation, or to placate the gods who lived above him, and even now in the closing years of the twentieth century the Chilterns attract religious and other cults far stranger than those of the modern Druids who still blow upon the Horn of Peace and cry to the rising sun from the Malvern hilltops. There are bodies of Chiltern worshippers who crowd deserted summits in order to become part of them, and to attract visitors from other planets in unidentified flying objects. There are said to be Covens of Chiltern witches, and there most certainly are many adherents of Straight Track and Sight Line theories, all based on the megalithic yard of 2·72 feet. All these people are convinced that Megalithic man was capable of naked-eye observations in these latitudes of a kind quite certainly impossible today. They know that a Holy Place was laid out at Wing, and that there were many other such places on which Christian churches have arisen, all on Sight Lines which in the dawn of history, they say, served astronomical and esoteric purposes. It is pleasant to reflect upon these matters as one drives about the Chilterns, particularly as they have again found champions among those who believe in the existence of 'leys', those mysterious (and, to the cynic, non-existent) lines described in John Michell's book, *The View Over Atlantis*, and which believers think are, 'a web of lines linking the holy places and sites of antiquity. Mounds, old stones, crosses and old cross roads, churches placed on pre-Christian sites, legendary trees, moats and holy wells all stood in exact alignments that ran over beacon hills to cairns and mountain peaks.' Fascinating stuff and easy to accept in some of those deep Chiltern woods in which the most sophisticated of visitors begins to feel apprehensive, and to experience the common sensation of being watched. The pattern of woodland and hill has everywhere had this effect on mankind, as readers of Sir James Frazer and other writers about early beliefs and rituals will know, but the Chilterns continue to provide a breeding ground for strange woodland beliefs where elsewhere in England they have died out with disafforestation.

But there are more tangible objects; and all of them worth seeing. It is typical of what has happened to the southern escarpment of the Chilterns that the Cook memorial in Chalfont St. Giles can only be seen after application to the Coal Board, but it is well to remember that nearly everything in the present-day world is better imagined than seen. This is not true of great pictures, of great mountains and the great natural views spread over the world, but of objects now engulfed in the buildings and motorways of the twentieth century it is certainly true. The 'Ship Money record of claim' in Great Kimble church is a small example of this. Here is a document which altered our history, curbed the powers of the Monarchy, plunged our country into Civil War. And now it hangs on the wall of the church, in an ordinary picture frame, as uninspiring as any 'Stag at Bay'. But it must be seen for all that.

As should many other objects in the area which derive their present interest from the passage of time. In a quarter of a century this writer has never seen anyone pause at the pillar standing where the road to Princes Risborough and Aylesbury leaves the Oxford/London road shortly before West Wycombe village. It has been there for a long time, having been set up by Sir Francis Dash-wood, the first Lord le Despenser, to mark the completion of his new road with materials excavated from and forming the caves and galleries underneath the church at West Wycombe. 'To the City', reads the inscription, 'To the University. To the County Town'.

There is another of these Chiltern marker pillars, of even greater interest—the Obelisk at the entrance to Marlow. At one time this formed the 36th milestone on 'The Salisbury Gout Track', as the private short cut made by the Cecil family through Marlow to the Bath road at Reading came to be called. Although the whole venture was primarily for the convenience of the family and was designed to ameliorate some of the agonies of a slow horse-drawn expedition 'to the waters' by gout-wracked patients, this was a public-spirited piece of road improvement. Enough toll gates were provided to produce an income in excess of £2,000 a year until the coming of the railways. There are still a few of these toll houses left in the Chilterns, notably a fine specimen at the London end of High Wycombe. This was 'let' for £3,500 a year until the railway was built, every coach except the Mail having to pay toll on journeys from London to Oxford, Gloucester and the West.

Nearly everything of this kind is overlooked by the motorist; there simply is not time to notice that a simple brick building (like the High Wycombe toll house) is out of the ordinary and worth a pause. As another example of a seldom visited curiosity, the mound by the war memorial in Latimer is the grave of a horse, or perhaps the heart and trappings of a horse. The animal was wounded in the Boer War and his rider (General de Villebois Mareuil) was killed saving the life of Lord Chesham, of Latimer House. There are of course standard 'sights' like the Disraeli graves in Hughenden churchyard, the wood carvings in Hambleden church, and scores of others, which can only be visited on foot, but everywhere in the Chilterns a great deal is perforce missed every day by the hurrying motorist.

Chiltern footpaths have become a subject in themselves, and the Chiltern Society has made itself responsible for surveying and issuing particulars of no less than 3,204 of them, comprising hundreds of miles of quiet walking in high and wooded places. There is now a footpath observer in practically every village in the Chilterns and a voluntary clearing force, working always in harmony with landlords and farmers, in excess of 300 people. The bird-watcher and the observer of shy and rare animals in the Chilterns now finds his path literally of the easiest.

Of course, walking in the Chilterns, the subject of a special chapter, has become less easy since the almost total abolition of Chiltern railways. In the '80s and '90s of last century, when walking in England as a pastime was at its height, it was a simple matter to take a train from say Oxford to Thame or Princes Risborough, to walk from there to Goring and to return the same evening by train. Such a walk today would require a co-ordinator and a waiting motor-car at the terminal point. Thus Chiltern walks now tend to become round trips and to be shorter, which is really in the English tradition. This was never a country of walkers, the first mention of 'a walk' in English fiction being that taken by Miss Elizabeth Bennett in *Pride and Prejudice*. The fantastic walks in most of Dickens' books are figments of the imagination. No one ever walked from the City to Richmond and back in order to lunch with the 'Little Dorrit' Meagleses, or did 25 miles on a dark Christmas afternoon between a late and drunken breakfast and an early dinner at Dingley Dell. In the great days of Chiltern walking it was very much an occupation for dons and schoolmasters, an opportunity for learned debate or amicable discussion.

Finally, on any sightseeing expedition the Chiltern visitor should keep in his mind the *newness* of most of the place names. Admittedly this is a highly specialised subject, there are literally hundreds of volumes by scores of writers devoted to it, but here in the Chilterns there is a different 'feel' to the names from those of the more ancient settlements in say Kent. Nearly all the Chiltern names are post-Norman Conquest, many of them much later than that. This serves to emphasise the always sparsely populated nature of the country. The Chilterns as an area to be enjoyed, to be lived in, to be returned to at night from distant work places were almost unknown until the turn of the nineteenth century. The names of the villages reflect this peaceful obscurity.

CHAPTER SIX

Farms and Woodlands

It is natural to turn from a consideration of Chiltern places and objects of interest to a brief account of the land surrounding them. How did it come to be arranged as it is; what use is made of it now?

It has been said already that prehistoric man found the Chilterns unattractive as a dwelling place. There is some evidence of early human life along the general line of the Icknield Way, and prehistoric finds have been made in the gravels between Henley and Mapledurham, but bones or domestic 'finds' of any sort are rare. The Chilterns must have been harsh country indeed as the ice cleared away and the grass and the trees began. There are some Bronze Age barrows around the Princes Risborough Gap, and there are plenty of Roman remains, of a sort. There are still evidences of the Saxons, but the general contribution of man in the Chilterns has always been small right through the ages, even the coming of the railroads having little effect on the remoter parts of the area. It is the motor-car which has brought new populations to the unbroken farmlands of the past. It is also the motor-car and the special roads prepared for it which on the one hand has made certain formerly easy journeys dangerous and difficult, and on the other has drained the traffic from numerous small roads and lanes. It is for example a rather dangerous and time-wasting motor drive from Hughenden Manor to Windsor Castle, taking much longer than in the days when Disraeli, as Prime Minister, made it behind two good horses through open country. But with a little care and a good map it is also possible to drive about all day in Chiltern country in almost traffic-free conditions.

The existing pattern of settlements and villages, as we know them today, was largely fixed in the Chilterns before the time of Domesday Book in 1088, but there were then two vast forests which prevented any large-scale development: the Royal Forest of Windsor, covering most of what is now east Berkshire, and Bernwood, now completely disafforested, which covered all the land towards Oakley and Brill. Thus the main Chiltern settlements were controlled as to general plan and development by the run of the hills. None of this is now discernible south-eastwards of the southern escarpment. Urban man has obliterated the landscape.

But there was a special Chiltern way of life and, in considering it, some brief reference must be made to early cultivation systems. Until the enclosures of the fifteenth and sixteenth centuries an open-field system of farming was practised. This developed from the feudal system and is very much a cause of present-day English class consciousness. Briefly and not altogether accurately, but correct enough for discussion purposes, the system was one of shared grazing rights among the peasantry, who carried out crop cultivations in personal strips on commonly-held arable land.

In the beginning much of the profit from these operations went to the feudal master in the same way as the profits of share croppers today in other parts of the world. The overlord provided security and expected a return for it in crops and personal service. So, later on, did the landowner who offered the use of his land to farmers for a consideration. Both systems became riddled with corruptions and abuses, but both worked and were, on the whole, suited to the economic conditions and political situations of the times.

The great land enclosures brought the open-field system quite speedily to an end. Outside Aylesbury there lies the village of Quarrendon which can now be picked out only from the air. The whole village was eliminated by enclosure towards the end of the fifteenth century, but the main village street and the marks of communal farming are still faintly to be seen. That was how the Settlement and Enclosure Acts worked. When land was given to some great personage villagers were evicted from it, quite often as time went on, being settled elsewhere and, with reasonable compensation, in an atmosphere of goodwill. The effect of these arrangements in the Chilterns was that by the end of the eighteenth century the Chiltern pattern looked as though it dated from the earliest times and was, moreover, eternal. In that context it is worth bearing in mind that when Queen Victoria came to the throne, a sixth of England was owned by less than 100 people and that nearly all the Buckinghamshire Chilterns were in a single hand.

The orderly developments from that situation, a gradual transition from tenant farming to owner occupation, have been much disturbed in recent years. Some villages and their surrounding farmlands have been turned into considerable townships in the period since the Second World War, and some tracts of countryside have become vast aggregations of human beings which are neither villages or planned settlements but collections of houses set down where they can most easily be reached by motor-car. These are labelled with the name of the district in which they occur, but they are remote from them.

So much for the general picture of causes and effects; but it is what is happening now, and why, which is of interest to the Chiltern visitor or newly arrived resident. All the open country and all the timbered areas are of course 'farmed' in one way or another. There are a few commons, no longer serving their ancient purpose, and some heaths still proving unfit for any purpose; but most of the Chilterns, apart from the glories of the beechwoods is given over to the production of milk and those ancillaries of dairy farming everywhere, pigs and poultry. As in the past the higher lands are given up to sheep. The main picture is obscured a little in the Chilterns by the high incidence (at present) of hobby farming, tax-loss farming, part-time farming and, more recently, what can only be described as 'bungalow farming'. Some Chiltern farmers, especially those on the outskirts of growing settlements, are yielding to the fat cheque books and blandishments of the developers. Who is to blame them?

There was, in the late 1950s, a minor revival of high arable farming in the Chilterns. This was the short day of the so-called Barley Barons, but once again dairy farming is all-pervading (with the exceptions listed above). Farming in the Chilterns, as elsewhere, is at present inside another long cycle of poor returns for big efforts and permanent grass has always been the only answer to that. The growth of London has forced the really high arable men, the market gardeners, further and further away from their main point of sale, leading to a considerable expansion from the small beginnings of market gardening between Slough and Maidenhead in the 1920s. There is some specialised fruit growing, although the cherry orchards, once a common sight all over the Chilterns and thought to be the best of all long-term agricultural investments are gradually dying out. There are still some commercial orchards and, outside the little towns, the usual plant and shrub nurseries, but taken as a whole the dairy cow is queen of the Chilterns and likely to remain so for many years.

The mechanics of all this have changed greatly, altering the general look of the countryside. There is a marked tendency towards larger holdings created by purchase or amalgamations and everywhere a stripping out of hedges to ease the movements of tractors and big machines. This is not altogether the disaster feared by observers, the hedge as such being a comparative newcomer to the English scene, and largely the outcome of the savagely penal Game Laws of the late eighteenth century and onwards. As recently as 1845 the iniquity of the game-preserving hedgerows insisted upon by landlords was the subject of a lecture to the Farmers' Club. There were ten parishes in Devon, said Mr. Knight, the lecturer, in which there were 36,000 acres of hedgerow trees, enough to stretch for 1,651 miles, or half as long again as the Great Wall of China. Now in the Chilterns, as elsewhere, the hedges are coming down for the convenience of groups of farmers who are sharing their equipment and buying ever larger machines in the interests of economy. Things change all the time in England but so slowly that no one generation grasps the fact of change. 'No one makes history,' wrote Boris Pasternak, 'no one sees it happen, no one sees the grass grow.'

There is much so-called amenity land in the Chilterns, made essential because of the density of the new populations. The whole area is now well provided with parks, golf courses, playing fields, all highly valuable 'lungs' as they are called, but all taking land out of food production. One of the prices to be paid by increasing populations is in the higher cost of food, a lesson not yet grasped in an England accustomed to thinking and voting in terms of cheap food for the best part of 200 years.

The woodlands are changing. Still marginally profitable in the hands of enlightened owners, the beechwoods of Japan are beginning to cast the same kind of long shadow over them as did the prairies of North America over the English tenant farmer in the great days of high corn prices. But the woods persist. They can be seen from every Chiltern road, indeed most of the Chiltern roads run through them. They are the principal attraction of the area and the glory of it. In the autumn all the Chilterns are on fire, the wooded hills glowing richly brown, red, and, at last yellow. In the spring the soft green of the beechwoods joins with the daffodils to take the winds of March with beauty. Some of the woodlands are now purely decorative, having been clear-felled long ago, a fringe of trees spared as a straightforward preservation of amenity. But there is expert agreement that the unique Chiltern proliferation of trees will continue through the foreseeable future. The nature of the territory will ensure that. On all such matters there is also a new public conscience which appears to be strengthening daily.

Whole books have been devoted to descriptions and considerations of the Chiltern heathlands, but now they have almost gone, much of the remaining heaths being safe in institutional hands or held within the National Trust. It is surprising that the 'commoner' owners of many of the smaller patches of Chiltern Heath are quite unknown and that in some cases no one on a parish or rural district council can tell what control may or may not be exercised, or even in numerous cases, where.

Finally, we must take into account the sad view of Professor Coppock that the influence of Greater London on the Chilterns will not diminish but is likely to grow. It is difficult to contest this most expert opinion particularly bearing in mind the new stream-lined train services, the widespread driving of new roads, the truly alarming increases in the birthrate, set against the acute shortage of 'London' building land; and the growing prosperity of all those industries which can flourish in rural surroundings. As recently as 1958 the National Parks Commission designated the Chilterns as officially 'An Area of Outstanding Natural Beauty'. Much of horror has been perpetrated since then, but there is a growing tendency everywhere in the Chilterns to curb the wilder excesses of the developers and expansionists. The industries, which we are now to examine, are not in themselves destructive but are based on the geology and ecology of the area and run by Chiltern men. All that is needed by farmers, by manufacturers and by the existing residents is a period of time, based on stop orders and moderate restrictions, which will enable solutions to be found for the multiplicity of human problems that threaten to overwhelm certain parts of the Chiltern country.

13   *A little-changed backwater on the river near Cookham*

CHAPTER SEVEN

Chiltern Industry

Everywhere in England the land and the environment have produced the local industry. As coal and iron in the industrial north,
so from the limestone hills and the beechwoods flourishing upon
them, the cement and furniture industries of the Chilterns grew.
The chalk has been worked in the Chilterns since the beginning, the
Romans enlarging the pits they found to produce the lime for their
special form of concrete. Those early pits at Chinnor and Pitstone
are now vast automated cement works eating steadily into the
hills which shelter them. It is easy to deplore that; to write and
talk of despoliation, the dangers of dust and fumes, the desolated
horror of the worked out areas. But to what end? There has to be
cement if the western way of life is to continue, and it must be got
where the steep hills flatten to chalk beds under the stiffest of
clays, enabling the simplest form of surface mining to be carried
on. The communities which suffer from this form of industry are
few in number and are expected to suffer in silence for what is
always described in similar circumstances as the greatest good of
the greatest number.

Far more important is the furniture industry of the Chilterns,
which grew directly from the wooded countryside. The beech is
not found in its Chiltern abundance anywhere else in the British
Isles, and the beech is a hardwood, wonderfully adapted to the
manufacture of chair-legs and backs, table-legs and, in its less
perfect forms, all those parts of furniture unseen or covered by
richer timber veneers.

Well inside living memory the Chiltern 'bodgers' set up their
woodland huts, or sat in the doorways of their conveniently sited

cottages to turn out endless supplies of chair-legs, struts, chair-backs, and supports. Their hand-scrapers, foot-lathes, oil-lamps and heavy frieze coats are all museum pieces now and any surviving 'bodgers' are in peaceful retirement. But the industry which gave work to these men, whose raw materials were the beechwoods, flourishes as never before, with High Wycombe still at the centre of affairs as it has been for centuries. There can hardly be a house in this country without some example of woodwork from the Chiltern hills.

Most of the timber used in the modern furniture industry is no longer produced locally. In the timber yards scattered through the area may be seen plunder from the forests of the world; French plane trees, Guyanan teak, veneers from California or the swamps of the Amazon, coffin wood from Sussex or the Baltic. But every factory in High Wycombe, still has its third- or fourth-generation craftsmen, bred to the woodworking traditions of the Chilterns. The names over many of the factory gates may be matched in the churchyards of the surrounding villages. It may now cost a hundred pounds a day to keep a bandsaw running in a timber yard where, a generation or so back, a few men in sawpits did identical work, a thousand times more slowly, for subsistence wages. But the men on the bandsaw are mostly descended from the men in the sawpit, with the same eye for knots and flaws as the yard owner, the same 'feel' for the natural line of the work. And the 'saw doctor' of today exercises the identical skills employed by his grandfather when saw setting, except that he uses modern tools working through a vastly greater number of teeth.

High Wycombe is the home of the Windsor chair, known throughout the world as an open-backed beechwood chair with an elm seat. Not even the furniture historians know how it came by its name, which has nothing to do with so late an arrival on the Windsor scene as Queen Victoria—Mr. Pickwick stood on a Windsor chair to make his first immortal speech at least five years before Queen Victoria came to the throne. Sir Laurence Weaver has suggested that the first Windsor chairs may have come from Windsor forest, but in the form that everyone knows it the chair has been made in High Wycombe for the best part of 200 years. James Gomme was making it, and much other beautiful furniture, on the site of the present Gomme factory as long ago as 1798. He was the man who introduced the Bucks Shilling, bearing his name and the date 1811, a token coin redeemable at any High Wycombe shop for 12 pennyworth of goods. There are still a few of them to be found or seen here and there. By 1874 it was estimated that a million and a half chairs were made annually in High Wycombe, seven chairs a minute throughout the year. Today every kind of furniture is produced there, most of it by machines in giant fully-automated factories. But there is still a surprising amount of hand-work in all but the simplest articles.

Until quite recently there was a great deal of life in the Chiltern woodlands, people and animals moving about among the trees, disturbing and distributing the beech 'mast', treading it into the ground with heel and hoof. That is all over, gone with the axemen, the cross-cut sawyers, and, 'the bravest sight in all the world', the six or eight shire horses in line dragging out the felled timber on the heavy 'tugs' of the day. Now the pig, which at the time of the Conquest roamed the woods and forests as a semi-wild creature, is being brought into the woods again to keep up the essential scuffling and turning, burying and raking.

With the hand-working foresters have gone the ancillary industries of the Chiltern woods, lacemaking and the keeping of ducks. There is no need of cottage industries when the man of the house gets big wages for operating a machine saw capable of felling 120 years of growth in 50 seconds. All that remains of the pillow-lace industry are the high-priced boxwood bobbins in the antique shops, and of the ducks an occasional deserted and stagnant village pond, the focus of complaints from new residents or of new parish councillors eager to make a mark.

There is still a big demand for English beech, but the trade is dwindling and after many centuries a distant end to hardwood forestry in England is becoming visible. There are now Chiltern factories which use not a single British log in their entire output. It is said that the French and the Japanese, indeed the foresters of almost any country except our own, will grade their timber; that a buyer in High Wycombe can order his requirements across the world by grade number and know exactly what he will in due course receive. It is said that English growers admit to the existence of one grade only, 'Excellent', and that deliveries all too often fail to reach that standard. Happily that is not the whole story.

All around High Wycombe there are big village timber-yards in which the raw materials of the furniture trade are prepared for the factories. In the huge Siarey yard in Chinnor there are stacks from all over the world of afrormosia, African walnut, mahogany, almost anything which grows as a tree. But here, too, from the West Wycombe and other Chiltern forest estates come the giant English beech logs to be split into 'boules', stacked in the open until fit enough to be kiln-dried, and eventually squared down and made ready for the smaller machines which fashion the wood into any shape or form for which there is a demand. It is these rough chair-legs, and backs, chair- and sofa-frames, table-legs and tops which go off to the furniture manufacturer to be made up into the veneered, polished, upholstered, finished article. Only the very biggest factories do all the work for themselves. The long preliminaries of seasoning and preparing need the lower-cost space of the villages; a timber buyer walking through the endless aisles of the Siarey yard can pick and choose, state his requirements, and depart satisfied. It is then that he may permit himself the reflection that Chinnor, that unlovely over-developed village still preserves an industry which it has nurtured through the centuries, from the 700-year-old screen in the parish church to the new oak timbers in the roof at Ewelme.

Enough has been said to show that the Chiltern woodlands are by no means pleasure grounds, happily located for the benefit of picnic parties and young lovers, although there is much woodland where both are welcome. But mostly the woodlands are most carefully worked backgrounds to the agricultural scene, and very much a part of it. There are still plenty of skilled woodsmen, not so picturesque as they were once, but with all the knowledge required for the exercise of an infinite patience, an ability to gauge correctly the times and places for the operations of thinning, pollarding, under planting and the like, and an awareness of all the dangers at felling times. With this knowledge properly applied, the long slow rotation of the beech crop, 60, 70, 100, up to 120 years, according to the requirements of the trade, may be so managed as to bring livelihoods to present owners and workers alike, together with some reasonable hopes for their posterity. Fewer men will be needed in the woodlands, but there will always have to be men of the trees while the Chilterns last. There is no fortune waiting for anyone in those superb hanging woods, but they are going to be there for a long time yet.

And that despite an entirely new Chiltern industrial feature, the arrival in great variety of the so-called 'light' industries, especially the light engineering trades which are best carried on in rural areas of cheap land with an ample supply of male and female labour. Such industries in the Chilterns are suitably placed to serve the whole country, without the expenses and conditions of the Black Country or the environs of Birmingham. Thus on the outskirts of High Wycombe the Cressex Estate begins to rival Slough; Saunderton, a tiny village in 1950 is now a flourishing industrial area. Suburban Oxford has more industry to show than its giant motor works, as have Dunstable and Hitchin. The industrialist is moving into Thame, having doubled the population of Aylesbury in 15 years. Any factory, anywhere, will attract residents to work in it; the whole of industrial England bears witness to that. There are now big Chiltern settlements created by the hope of secure livelihoods on regular wages. There they are with their grand or evocative array of street names, set down in huge blocks of one pattern at a reasonable, or at least payable, price on a 25-year mortgage. Each dwelling has a patch of garden, plenty of garage space, a washing machine, part central heating and a suggestion that there has been created a rainbow-touched fairyland, a romantic Greenery Street, almost a Valhalla for young gods, practically given away in a single package for the skilled workman, the junior technologist, and the rising young executive. The problems raised in the Chilterns by these new industries and the men and women drawn to them are formidable, and mostly outside the scope of this book. No provision is ever made by developers for the educational needs of the children to be born on their sites. No one has as yet seen an advertisement reading, 'We have even thought of a school in sun-drenched Pleasantville' although 'educational facilities' sometimes occurs, as a meaningless and misleading phrase. As there is no provision in the houses themselves for old people, Old People's Homes have become a feature of new developments. These, naturally, are sited on the cheaper land, far away from shops, churches, the branch of the county library, or any recreational centres.

There are indications that many of the new young Chiltern people have no intention of putting down roots, of staying too long in one place. They do not in any case think of themselves as living in the Chilterns, but as 'living where my husband can get to work easily' or, 'where it's cheap and convenient; it wasn't convenient in Acton where we've come from'.

It would be absurd not to recognise that the entire Chiltern area is under stress, with the new men and women different in every way from those of earlier generations. Their very work is a mystery not to be properly understood by anyone over the age of 50. They are not in the main church goers, certainly they are not committed church members; this in itself cuts them off from the old centres of village unity stemming from church and chapel. They are mostly unattracted by the Womens' Institutes, Mothers' Unions, Fellowships of one sort or another. They are, men and women alike, specifically 'non-joiners'. That is the phrase they will use if questioned. There are contradictions to set against that. Surprising eruptions of Bach Choirs, Little Theatres, discothèques, poetry-reading groups, model-making clubs, and everywhere there is Bingo.

These activities have split the Chiltern villages. The Flower Show is for the older residents, the public house has been compelled to adopt a new 'image' in which only the eternal cheesecake of the cigarette and drink advertisements remains of the old 'local'. Times have changed indeed. The picturesque in the Chilterns, as elsewhere, has nearly always meant dirt, and the newcomers will have none of it. Their lives are based on getting away as often as possible for as long as possible from the communities in which they live, and they have all the labour-saving dirt-dispelling machinery to make that possible. Not for them hours with mop and scrubbing brush; they are living in the Golden Age which was promised to them. They know it and are enjoying it. They have already diminished the endless child-bearings which for a few years marked their increased leisure and affluence, and it is possible that by the end of the next decade, as the hastily formulated plans now being made for Chiltern babes in their perambulators approach fruition, the whole Chiltern population may have become stable. Everything in the last few pages may be taken in at a glance by comparing, side by side, a photograph of the First World War period of poorly clothed children in a village school, with a group of primary school children of today running gaily out to greet the car-borne parents awaiting them.

There is only one other point which need be considered here. The whole outlook of parents under 40 (and thus of their children) is different from anything ever before experienced not only in this country or in the Chilterns but in the world. Elders speak loosely of a Technological Age, but they hardly know what they are saying; they cannot comprehend that an entire civilisation has changed with the computer, the move into space, the satellite spy, the intercontinental missile, the actual enlargement of a world which until 30 years ago was thought to be growing steadily smaller. The day of the business letter is over and with it the need for literate clerks. We live in an age of the printed form, the unconfirmed unfiled telephone call, the 'convenience' meal, manipulated views from cameras which have learned to lie. We have lived, those of us who have left 50 behind, through a revolution which has filled every mental home in the country to bursting point with men and women who cannot adjust to the new pressures. We have forgotten that it was only children at first who could understand the 'cats whisker' when wireless as entertainment burst upon mankind, and that it is only the young who comprehend the miracles of today. This situation seems to exist with peculiar force in the Chilterns of the last 20 years. There is a desire for something which cannot be found here, perhaps could not exist here, entertainment, excitement, variety. But the Chilterns, as a whole are still holding the twentieth century at a distance. They may well provide a haven in the twenty-first.

CHAPTER EIGHT

Chiltern Footpaths

It is pleasant to leave the industry of the Chilterns, and a consideration however brief of some of the sociological factors affecting present-day life in the area, and to get back to the countryside itself. We need not again concern ourselves with other than the delights of the Chiltern scene.

The footpaths and bridleways first. There are over 3,000 of them in the Chiltern area, all properly surveyed, all amicably and properly agreed between owners, parish councils and other interested parties. The prime mover in this work has been and is the Chiltern Society, a body which after only a few years of existence has already attracted some 1,500 paid-up members and associates, acquiring thereby considerable power and influence in the preservation of amenity in matter-of-fact, twentieth-century, ways. For footpath survey purposes, the Society divided the Chilterns into seven areas, each of which is invigilated by responsible members to prevent accidental ploughing out, or in a few cases the deliberate closing of footpaths and bridleways which have a clear Right of Way based on immemorial custom or other valid considerations.

The main difficulty of footpath preservation and maintenance in modern times and present-day conditions is that all of them originally served the purely local requirements of nearby residents. They were a way to the church, or from the village to the allotments, or to the various licensed premises of the district. Many of them, indeed, still serve those purposes, but the footpath network as a whole is not at all suitable for 'round turn' walking over any distance from car, through open countryside, and back to

86

car, or at least not without much retracing of steps. To try and remedy this situation, without in any way interfering with the rights of property owners and other land users, has been the difficult task of the Chiltern Society in recent years. A system called the Radial System based on the linkage of footpaths around villages has been worked out, which permits a few walks from car back to car of 15 miles or more and a great number of family strolls taking an hour or so to return to starting point.

The density of Chiltern footpaths is surprising, and far higher than anywhere else in England. Mr. Don Gresswell, an acknowledged footpath authority and the Chairman of the Chiltern Society Rights of Way group, has calculated that (in the heart of the Buckinghamshire Chilterns) in the Wycombe and Amersham Rural Districts there are four miles of public footway for every square mile of area. In the nearby Vale of Aylesbury there are only just over three miles of path to the square mile, and at Wing, just clear of the Chilterns, only two and a half miles. The main cause of this is the narrow folded nature of the Chiltern landscape which has always limited the construction of laneways and secondary roads.

A great deal remains to be done. The planned Ridgeway Walk, a miniature Chiltern version of the Pennine Way, or the newly surveyed and opened Welsh trackway, Offa's Dyke, will not always follow the summits of the ridges, as it should, because the paths and roadways simply are not there or in some cases where they formerly existed have long been closed. It is said that to reach the top of Cymbeline's Mount a technical trespass must now be made, as also in the case of Pulpit Hill. It is of the utmost importance that users of the countryside bear in mind that even in apparently deserted areas 'something is going on' of extreme importance to the owner of that land. Nothing should be left on it; nothing dug up and taken away, nothing disturbed (in the case of livestock), or frightened. There is a Country Code which spells all this out and it should be followed at all times. Whole footpath networks can be imperilled by a single picnic party forgetting the first maxim of all country dwellers, 'You brought it with you; take it home.' This is not facile preaching; observance of the Country Code is absolutely vital to the continued living existence of the Chiltern footpath network.

For 90 per cent of Chiltern visitors the existing footpaths are more than adequate. This is not serious walking country compared with say North Wales, the Pennines and Lake Districts, or the highlands of Western Scotland. The average motorist in the Chilterns wants to enjoy the peace of the country and to stretch his legs in comfort. This is now possible everywhere in the area, all the routes being properly and clearly marked. It has become necessary, and it is a valuable aid to inexperienced country ramblers, to put up small green arrows or to paint white arrows on trees wherever there is a danger that the true path might be overlooked or strictly private property invaded. By following these waymarks carefully the casual walker will enjoy himself, see much of great beauty and bring himself into no difficult situations.

It is on the footpaths of the Chilterns, rather than by the roadsides that the visitor may allow his mind to wander a little over the centuries and to reflect upon the various happenings in the villages, hamlets and townships all about him. The motorist is within ten minutes, at Princes Risborough, of nearly everything the Buckinghamshire Chilterns have to offer, but the wayfarer, standing above Whiteleaf Cross, finds himself surrounded by Roman remains and the vestiges of religious settlements of mediaeval times. Below him Princes Risborough lies on the Chiltern divisions of the Icknield Way, where the Black Prince had his castle. He will be on the spot where William the Conqueror was checked for a while in his invasion plans. He is in Chiltern beechwood and within two miles of the Forest Products Research Institute.

Across the valley on walks about and around Radnage, and indeed along the minor roads there, the visitor will find nearly everything of the peace which once characterised the whole Chiltern area. There is no traffic and he will have no company along the footpaths. The woodlands here are among the most beautiful in the country, clinging to the hillsides all the way down to the

A40 at West Wycombe. St. Christopher was always a considerable figure in the Chilterns, where travel was dangerous and
difficult, and here he is again in the little Radnage church which
should not be missed, standing back from and above the narrow
village road.

Whatever footpath routes are chosen a walk along at least a part
of the Grimsditch should not be omitted. In many places all that remains is remarkably like an overgrown hedge and ditch anywhere in England, but a few minutes spent in a stroll along the top
of the real thing, perhaps where it runs across the Icknield Way
hard by the A4130 Henley/Wallingford road, is a memorable
experience. A man on top of Grimsditch here may become his
own archaeologist, agreeing with or dissenting from the numerous
speculators who have preceded him.

There are miles and miles of completely unspoiled walking
country above and on both sides of High and West Wycombe,
which at first sight, and even on the map, looks uninviting. There
is, for example, a particularly beautiful very short walk from the
door of West Wycombe church through light woodlands down to
the Bledlow Ridge road. And amidst the intricate network of lanes
and secondary roads (all splendid for walkers) between Bradenham and the Hampdens, the explorer may chance to find himself
slaking a thirst at one of the most beautifully named public houses
in England, Rupert Brooke's celebrated 'Pink and Lily' at Speen.

Mr. Cadbury Lamb begins his little Chiltern book, *Discovering
Buckinghamshire* with the sentence: 'The real Chiltern Hills are
in Buckinghamshire.' The Chiltern walker may well dissent from
this. He might say, 'What about the four walks around Henley described by the Chiltern Society?' One of these, from Nettlebed to Bix and thence through woodlands to a spot 400 yards from
the start, can be done in an hour and will convey the essence of
the Chilterns to the walker. Incidentally it may fill his mind with
doubts about his easy acceptance of the Wessex/Mercia frontier
theory while walking along the top of the Grimsditch. For here
on this walk the Ditch alters its character completely and is known
as Highmoor Trench.

Still away from Buckinghamshire it may be observed that there is nothing to touch the walks and strolls on or along any part of the superb summits between Chinnor and Watlington. The very names are an invitation: Pyrton Hill, Shirburn Hill, Bald and Beacon Hills, Kingston and Crowell Hills, and Chinnor Hill itself. The back road from Christmas Common to the A40 near Stokenchurch takes a wonderful line between the woodlands and the hills, and everywhere along those few miles there are parking places and picnic areas which, although they draw perhaps too many people in high summer, do much to preserve this lovely area from indiscriminate overrunning. In the spring along this road the visitor may still see Shirburn Wood azure with bluebells. In 1940 Massingham predicted that nothing whatever of beauty and interest would be left here within a decade. All is still reasonably well and safe.

There is a road, or lane rather (still in the Oxfordshire Chilterns), halfway between Nettlebed and Watlington which winds through Russells Water to Maidensgrove and eventually to Stonor. The visitor to Maidensgrove or any of the surrounding 'buried' villages of the Chilterns will be slow to admit the claims of Buckinghamshire to the sole possession of the true hills.

Nor for that matter will the Chiltern walker in Hertfordshire, anywhere between Aldbury and Little Gaddesden. He has Ashridge forest and the high walks (up to 700 feet) about Pitstone. Of course all the solitudes of the Chilterns must increasingly be sought farther and farther away from the southern escarpment and the outward spread of London. This is also becoming more and more true along the stretches of river marking the Thames Valley Chilterns. Henley is the centre, and between there and Marlow on one side and Caversham (on the Reading outskirts) on the other, the unceasing tide of traffic in spring and summer serves only to indicate that there must be something of special interest to reward the autumn or winter visitor. As indeed there is. That is the time to explore the inside of the Marlow/Cookham/Maidenhead river curve, and both banks of the Thames between Medmenham and Remenham.

The serious walker is not going to spend too much time on the footpaths of the Chilterns which, as we have seen, were not intended for recreation, but there is little to touch any footpath anywhere in the Chilterns for a leisurely stroll on a summer afternoon. The dedicated attempt which has been made to cater for the scores of thousands who drive into the Chilterns throughout the summer months should prove invaluable in the time immediately ahead when so much extra roadwork is under consideration for the whole area. It has not been easy for townspeople coming into the country to walk through the woods and across open fields. They have not known what to do or where it is permissible to go, and have had to be content to sit at roadsides by the parked car. Now things are better and such a visitor need envy no man as he embarks on a Chiltern adventure perhaps only three miles long, glancing at a leaflet which begins 'Start at Greys Green by the cricket field. Take the stile beside the old smithy. The path leads down through young trees to Rocky Lane.' And so on. There are 1,500 miles of these paths and bridleways in the Chilterns and never before has it been so easy and so pleasant to use them.

CHAPTER NINE

A Railway Journey
and Some Chiltern Walks

In beginning a description of numerous other short walks and drives in the Chilterns it is worth pointing out that it would have been possible until about 15 years ago to have made something of a comprehensive visual tour of the area by train. As it is, one unique railway introduction to the Chilterns survives, the line from Aylesbury to Marylebone, on the Stoke Mandeville/Wendover route. There is still some delightful Chiltern scenery between Princes Risborough and Beaconsfield on the main routes into Paddington or Marylebone, but the line along the southern escarpment shows what might have been and what, despite every kind of pressure, still remains. The pleasure is lost, somehow, on the journey *from* London; it is important to make it on the up-line.

There is first the remarkable stretch, without a curve, from Aylesbury, across the Vale to Stoke Mandeville and beyond; the line then crossing both Upper and Lower Icknield Ways before entering Wendover, to proceed along the southern escarpment to Amersham. A mile or so short of Great Missenden the Grimsditch is crossed. All this area is extremely heavily populated yet this is still very much a scenic line, the hills reaching to 600 and 700 feet all along the route, the beechwoods everywhere visible. Here is the true 'Metroland' line developed by the old Metropolitan Railway over London and North-Eastern tracks. This is the line which was conceived in order to bring Londoners into the country to live, and ended by bringing London itself there.

*14   Gateway to the Chilterns: Clarke's Bridge (1832) and Scott's
Steeple (1898) at Marlow*

A Railway Journey and Some Chiltern Walks

After Amersham the train runs through the Chalfonts, where the Chesham branch comes in, and on to the station for Latimer, going thence into London by Chorleywood and Harrow on the Hill. It is a short journey worth making for its own sake by anyone interested in Chiltern country. Every station (in pleasant weather) is an invitation to get out and walk. No traveller feels like that, on the alternative route, at Gerrards Cross, Beaconsfield or High Wycombe. Nothing else is left of railway importance, the fast G.W. route to Reading being uninteresting, and the Watlington/Princes Risborough line, with its lovely views all the way, has long been closed, as has the other scenic line from High Wycombe through Loudwater to Maidenhead. At one time there was also a beautiful line from Princes Risborough through Thame to Oxford, giving matchless Chiltern views at the beginning of the journey. But then as recently as 1950, Princes Risborough was a busy and important minor junction and not the commuter stop on single line working which it is today. There has never been any sort of railway communication in the 'secret' Chilterns west of Henley.

It has already been mentioned that the old serious walkers in the Chilterns used the railways where possible to get them to attractive starting points and home after long days on foot. That is no longer possible and there are now several guides and handbooks which base all their suggested walks and tours on the motorcar. These should be in the possession of every Chiltern explorer, together with large-scale maps for the footpath enthusiast. Here it is only possible to indicate a few routes employing roads for the most part, or only short excursions from the car. It will always help to wear the right sort of boots or shoes and to bear in mind that even in the simplest of hill country unexpected showers are common, as are the sudden mists dense enough for the novice or unheeding walker to lose his sense of direction. Light protective clothing is never out of place on a country walk.

Here then are some suggested walks:

1. *A Road Walk*. Leave Chinnor along the Princes Risborough

Road, (you will be on the Icknield Way), turning off for Bledlow Village with its Norman church. Skirt the manor house keeping to signs for Bledlow Ridge and either walk along this ridge for some while towards West Wycombe, or turn towards Chinnor for Chinnor Hill and a stroll along the summit of Crowell Hill to Spriggs Alley. This is basically a walk of about eight miles, Chinnor to Chinnor, but depending upon conditions it can be extended in any of three directions to ten or twelve miles. This is a walk entirely without difficulty, and without leaving a road, which demonstrates what Chiltern country can still be like in an area of rapid expansion and despite the only really unpleasant view of the great cement works, (looking down into it from the top of the hill).

2. *Car and Foot*. This takes in a short walk on top of the Grimsditch, but with the car more can be done. Cross the Henley/Wallingford road and park the car anywhere beyond Blenheim Farm. Stay on top of the Grimsditch until it runs out into open and almost deserted country. There is now no need for a fixed route as the whole scene invites a walk, and the car need never be more than half a mile or so away.

3. *The Perambulation of Ewelme*. It is not quite enough to park the car here and to take a quick look at the church. Take a little extra time and make the circuit of the village, which lies inside a network of lanes in such a way that your whole tour back to your car can be made in half an hour. That will give you a wonderful impression of the compact group—church, school and almshouses—in their incomparable setting.

4. *Christmas Common and a Stroll through the Woods*. Except in high summer there will be room for your car at the top of Watlington Hill, and several hundred acres of National Trust land in which to walk. Or take the short walk to the 'turn off' at Christmas Common and continue, this time on foot, to the A40 at Stokenchurch. This is another of the great Chiltern stretches, only

three or four miles, which has become perhaps a little too popular in recent years. The first few hundred yards will tell you why; the whole short route is enchanting.

5. *To Maidensgrove on Foot*. This is one of the most rewarding short walks in the Chilterns. Drive along B481 Nettlebed/Watlington to the sign 'Russells Water'. Leave the car here and follow signs through Russells Water and Maidensgrove to Stonor. Here the B480 may be joined which will bring the walker back to within a quarter of a mile from his starting-point. All the countryside around is at present isolated from the world, but the M4 extension on the route now determined may interfere with this peace, may even, some say, destroy it altogether, piercing as it will the only untouched ridge of the Chilterns and bisecting the village of Lewknor. But others say that the new road will ultimately be preservative, drawing off much traffic and eventually blending with the Chiltern background which, at first, it must seriously impair.

6. *Around Great Missenden*. This is unexpected Chiltern country of great charm. The best plan here is to drive from Princes Risborough to the Missendens, selecting any starting point which appeals. There will be dozens. The signposts must be the guides here, there being numerous attractive walks in the three or four miles between the Hampdens and Speen.

7. *The Icknield Way*. At least one walk should be taken along any characteristic stretch of the Green Road, for preference a section which was never developed by the Roman, Norman or later roadmakers. Lower Icknield Way from Aston Rowant into Chinnor at Mill Lane is exactly placed to give something of the 'feel 'attached to the entire Chiltern route of the Way (both Upper and Lower) from Dunstable to Goring. This short section is unfrequented, unspoiled at present by any buildings, and is level walking. A leisurely hour will suffice and among many other attractions, the walk unexpectedly displays Chinnor cement works set into the woods and hills like a cameo and lending support to a judgment

made more than once that viewed purely objectively, and as a group of buildings erected for a specific purpose, the cement works at Chinnor are as good an architectural feature as may be found within a ten-mile radius.

8. *In the Hertfordshire Chilterns.* The first choice must be the privacy (when sought) of Ashridge Forest. On a fine day in summer the verges will be densely packed with cars, but everywhere inside this magnificent National Trust property there are rides, walks, and footpaths which seem hardly frequented even at holiday times. The whole area is one of Chiltern playgrounds; the zoo at Whipsnade is not far away, there is the tree cathedral at Tring, also now in the hands of the National Trust, there is Pitstone Hill with the views which may be expected in these parts from 700 feet or so. There is Ivinghoe Beacon. The air may be full of gliders searching for their 'thermals' but here again is the Icknield Way coming in from Dunstable and across the Chess at Wigginton, there is yet another considerable fragment of the Grimsditch. All around there lies a Chiltern lane network, this one having its centre at Cholesbury, and radiating towards Aston Clinton, Wendover and Tring. Londonwards urbanisation begins almost at once.

9. *Around High Wycombe.* The growth of the town, from 17,000 to 77,000 in 20 years has almost destroyed the geographical heart of the Chilterns, but so persistent and protective are the woodlands that the walker can still recapture in many places that sense of complete isolation which he desires, particularly on the loop secondary road which begins (on the A40) about half-way between West Wycombe and Stokenchurch and makes its way to Lane End. There is still a village green at Stokenchurch, half a mile from the great roundabout on the A40, and from it some of the best and most deserted footpath walks in all the Chilterns start.

10. *The High Wycombe, Penn, Beaconsfield Enclosure.* In all these suggestions (they are nothing more; no habitual walker

wishes to be told where to go, still less how to make his way) there is an implication that the car should be left some distance from the main trunk routes. This is nowhere more necessary than around Penn. The village itself is dangerously close to the expansions of High Wycombe, but is being well preserved by the inhabitants. From several points around the walker may see Windsor Castle on a fine day and, sometimes, the grandstand at Ascot. These views give a fine understanding of Chiltern beauty, all the intervening country appearing unspoilt although, alas, it is not. Distance really lends enchantment here, and lends, too, additional emphasis to the steepness of the Chiltern ridges, nowhere round here reaching 650 feet but providing a sense of much uphill walking with rewards at the top of each stretch. This is very marked between High Wycombe and Naphill, all overbuilt, and with much for sorrow but not despair. For everything for which the Chilterns have always been renowned is still there, the woods and hills of course (this book is about them), but also the peace and quiet, the great unexpected deserted stretches, the absence of traffic as soon as the main routes are left, the innumerable churches, the silent indigenous inhabitants, the legends and traditions and above all, the endless falling away of the land into wooded dells and hedgelocked fields. It is in these things that the Chiltern walker delights and because of which every hour on foot in this countryside provides something to cherish in the mind.

CHAPTER TEN

The Chiltern Seasons

It should now be possible, the details of the area having been noted and explored in some depth, to look at the Chilterns as a whole and, after that, to indulge a few prejudices and a few enthusiasms; to review the seasons and their effects; even, perhaps, to make a few speculative extrapolations into the future on the graphs etched into the Chilterns of the present. And some of the people who lived here must not be forgotten.

A sketch map of the Chilterns somewhat resembles a carrot which has been laid (at an angle of 45 degrees) across the map of England between Luton and Pangbourne. The principal towns on the fringes of the carrot, and inside it, are, reading downwards, Luton, Dunstable, Tring, Berkhamsted, Wendover, Great Missenden, Chesham, Princes Risborough, Chalfont St. Giles. Then comes, at the heart of the carrot, High Wycombe, and, below it, Stokenchurch, Beaconsfield, Marlow, Watlington, Ewelme, Wallingford and Henley. The point of the carrot lies on the Goring Gap, between Goring and Pangbourne. It will be seen that five counties are involved, although tenuously in two cases : Berkshire and Bedfordshire cannot really be regarded as serious Chiltern contenders. The literature tends to confine itself to Buckinghamshire, with Oxfordshire a poor second. But a new prominence and a new sense of 'locality' is coming to the Oxfordshire hills, owing to the unspoilt nature of the valleys adjacent to the splendid Oxfordshire ridge of the Chilterns. In a little book, *Discovering the Chilterns*, J. H. B. Peel gives five motor tours, the longest 55 miles, which cover the entire area, and he realises that it is by motor-car that the Chilterns are going to be explored in the foreseeable future.

But that exploring motorist need not be on the move all the time; there are scores of places in which he will find it a delight to idle, to get the car off the road and to take a short walk. It is the greatest of pities that modern picnic practice mostly takes the form of sitting beside a motor-car at a roadside. It is not too important that this spoils the whole vista for fellow passing motorists, but the custom most sadly leaves a wealth of lonely lovely spots unvisited. This is not as it should be. Only a selfish minority desires to keep others from sharing country pleasures, a minority that equally deplores the crowds in front of great paintings, believing that its members alone fully understand the 'Primavera' in Florence or 'The Night Watch' in Amsterdam. The ideal surely is for all to be encouraged to enjoy their heritage, to wander harmlessly in deep country on footpaths and bridlepaths which have been there for centuries. How else can all of us learn the need for conservation and the proper use of the environment?

Spring and autumn are the perfect Chiltern seasons; in summer the roads are often uncomfortably crowded and many of the beauty spots unreachable. In winter the main reason for the sparsity of Chiltern populations over the centuries is all too apparent. But there is nothing more rewarding than a spring or autumn walk in a Chiltern wood. The nature of the beech tree which forms a high canopy on a clean trunk creates a forest floor almost entirely free from brushwood and other walking obstacles. But the casual visitor *must* in all wooded land confine himself most strictly to marked routes. Otherwise he may be trespassing or, worse, disturbing game. It cannot be stated too often that everything in the country belongs to someone, even the wild flowers and the hedgerows.

Areas for this kind of walking activity have already been suggested, but there is a circle, bounded by Marlow, Stokenchurch, Watlington, Nettlebed and Henley, within which everything can be found to delight the tourist, delay the motorist, interest the birdwatcher and botanist, and fill all the needs of the rambler. There are churches to be visited, antiquities to be studied, and one or two spectacular viewpoints; altogether a tiny paradise in autumn or spring. By the end of June the hedgerow flowers have gone and everything has taken on the thick deep greenness of the typical English countryside. The major glory of the beechwoods is still four months away.

Autumn is the time for the Chiltern fringes, the open country around Dunstable or Ipsden, the Vale of Aylesbury, the picture village of Long Crendon (not quite the vision it was 20 years ago), the little market town of Thame, already doomed to industrial expansion, the Oxford colleges, and the ancient churches at places like Wing and Waterperry. This is also the best time to make the tours suggested and mapped by Peel and the Titchmarshes.

The river towns are at their best in summer, but the crowds are uncomfortably great; as they are at that time everywhere. You may look undisturbed at the splendid unfinished, 'Christ Preaching at Cookham Regatta', in the Spencer Gallery in Cookham during March, but not during Marlow or Henley Regattas. Boulter's Lock on a Sunday morning is no longer a place of Edwardian grace and glamour, but the crowds are bigger and the girls just as pretty. There are people everywhere, motor-cars everywhere, and in the Chiltern summer it becomes necessary to develop the selective eye, that special tourist eye which takes in the glories of a building but not the hundred cars parked in front of it, that is rapt by the hanging beechwood and oblivious of the dozen picnic parties below it. It was a Chiltern man by adoption who wrote of Beaconsfield in 1909: 'Within a stone's throw of my house they are building another house. I am glad they are building it, and I am glad that it is within a stone's throw.' 'They' have built several hundred thousand houses in the Chilterns since G. K. Chesterton wrote that, and planned his 'massive and exhaustive sociological work in several volumes to be called "The Two Barbers of Beaconsfield" '. Alas that we never had it, but Chesterton foresaw the great crowds we have today just as 60 years earlier Wood of the Farmers' Club had foretold their coming. Neither man was afraid of them and neither must we be. We must adjust to them, but praying that they will try to avoid the narrow Chiltern roads in high summer.

In the autumn the Chiltern beechwoods match the New England maples in glory, everywhere vistas of gold and russet take and hold the eye. This is the time to look upward from the valleys, one such vantage point and perhaps one of the best, being from the train half-way between Princes Risborough and High Wycombe. Even better, it is the time to seek the hill roads and the highest points, clearing the tree tops. Drive now between Princes Risborough and Great Missenden; Chinnor to High Wycombe; Henley, through Nettlebed, to Watlington. The rewards are very great. The crowds have gone and the countryside is settling down to await the Chiltern winter.

The rains are usually incessant in December all over the Chilterns preceded by often dangerous and persistent November fogs. January is the snow month in Chiltern England, the hill-top roads and slopes often being impassable then. There is nothing for the visitor except the churches. These stand empty and usually cold, but winter is an excellent time for looking at those which are off the main track or, while as interesting as all old churches must be, are not worth a serious detour during a summer run. At Ivinghoe and Pitstone there are such churches, as there is at Bledlow, which, although a fourteenth-century building, shares with so many Chiltern churches that complete lack of 'compulsion' that attracts the visitor to, say, Ewelme. There is High Wycombe church, which may be taken with Keene's Guildhall and the Little Market hall attributed to the Adam brothers. There is a modern rood screen (by Sir Gilbert Scott, 1930) in Terriers church, High Wycombe. This will grow old most gracefully. Not far away in West Wycombe there is a modern church out of keeping with the flint and brick Buckinghamshire countryside, the Roman Catholic church of St. Mary and St. George.

Outside Buckinghamshire there is the oldest church in Europe (it is said) at Northchurch, and, on the Chiltern map, but not strictly a Chiltern building, a fine church at Drayton Beauchamp. In almost every village there is a church worth entering, but in all the Chilterns only a handful which can be regarded as treasure houses. All this countryside has a stern and abiding puritan tradition which led, in scores of instances, to long years of church neglect until the coming of the mid-Victorian restorers. They threw out much that would be preserved today and put in much that is rejected by modern taste. But not all modern and Victorian stained glass, for example, is bad, although many Chiltern churches seem to have got more than their share of the poorer examples, the Chiltern restorers as a whole lacking that intangible called 'taste'. But there was another side to the restorers and improvers which must not be forgotten. Chesterton, already once quoted, wrote for all the Chilterns at the time of the vexed controversy in Beaconsfield over the matter of a crucifix on the proposed memorial to the men of the First World War:

'Those who debated the matter were a little group of the inhabitants of a little country town; the rector and the doctor and the bank manager and the respectable tradesmen of the place, with a few hangers-on like myself of the more disreputable professions of journalism and the Arts. But the powers that were there in the spirit came out of all the ages and all the battlefields of history. Mahomet was there and the Iconoclasts who came riding out of the East to ruin the statues of Italy, and Calvin and Rousseau and the Russian anarchs and all the older England that is buried under Puritanism; and Henry III ordering the little images for Westminster and Henry V, after Agincourt, on his knees before the shrines of Paris. If one could really write the history of that little place, it would be the greatest of historical monographs.'

That or something like it could be written of every Parochial Church Council or School Managers Board, or Parish Council in the late twentieth-century Chilterns. There are ten years of research awaiting anyone aspiring to write a monograph about the smallest village.

CHAPTER ELEVEN

Some Chiltern People

There is always a temptation to link the work of artists with their place of residence, finding actual towns and villages in Hardy's Wessex and Trollope's Barsetshire, but there is not much in it. Stanley Spencer's work was influenced by Cookham it is true, but John Piper lives in the Chilterns without there being any noticeable Chiltern influences in his painting. And so it is with most of the people who have lived and worked in this part of the world.

It has been claimed that Geoffrey Chaucer lived in the Chilterns for a time, but the only evidence for that is the grave of his son Thomas in the church at Ewelme. Perhaps Geoffrey visited him there. But among the poets, Shelley, Edmund Waller, Thomas Gray, Walter de la Mare, G. K. Chesterton, and possibly the great Milton all produced some of their work while living or staying in Chiltern country. Masefield may have written his 'Everlasting Mercy' in Great Hampden. There is, however, no recognisable school of Chiltern poetry, and the constant association of Rupert Brooke with the area is based on a reference to Wendover in his sad poem about finding a new girl, 'a better one than you, and I daresay she will do', and four lines of doggerel in the bar of the 'Pink and Lily' at Speen. Brooke was very much an East Anglian man.

The legend of Milton finishing *Paradise Lost* and beginning *Paradise Regained* in the Chilterns is entirely without foundation. The so-called 'Milton's Cottage' in the Chalfonts was never his, but Thomas Ellwood's, and Milton was only in it for a short time. Thomas Ellwood thought of himself as a Chiltern poet, but his

work has not lived and we look on him now as a Quaker buried at
Jordans who provided a refuge for Milton during part of the
Great Plague.

Gray lived in Stoke Poges and is buried and remembered there.
But although his Elegy may have been conceived in the churchyard there, and some of it actually written there too (Gray
polished the poem for years), the immortal lines, as Johnson
wrote, 'abound with sentiments to which every bosom returns an
echo'. Stoke Poges will always be a place of pilgrimage while the
English language lasts, but the pilgrim of today will find little to
hold him and much to speed him elsewhere. Edmund Waller,
buried in Beaconsfield churchyard, was a genuine Chiltern man,
born at Coleshill, his uncle being the great John Hampden, mortally wounded at Chalgrove Field and dying in Thame.

Shelley wrote at least part of *The Revolt of Islam* while staying in Marlow, and perhaps Chesterton had the Icknield Way in
mind when one of his characters in *The Flying Inn*, declaiming
his version of the Road to Roundabout under what he called
a great disadvantage, 'since I *know* why the road curves about'
said,

> *And I was told by Doctor Low*
> *Whom Mr. Wimpole's aunt would know*
> *Who lives at Oxford writing books*
> *And ain't so silly as he looks*
> *The Romans did that little bit*
> *And we've done all the rest of it.*

But those are tenuous links indeed. It has been claimed that Sir
Walter Scott named his *Ivanhoe* after being impressed by Ivinghoe Beacon, the place at that time being commemorated by a
doggerel about 'Tring, Wing, and Ivanhoe'. There cannot be any
substance in such a claim, or no more than that Rubbra's music or
that of Miss Freda Swayne is all Chiltern inspired, or that A. E.
Coppard drew the material for his short stories and poems from
his Chiltern surroundings. On those grounds the Chilterns could

most certainly claim Mr. Graham Greene, who was born and brought up in Berkhamsted, or *Dream Days* because Kenneth Grahame spent his retirement in Pangbourne. Pope had romantic associations with the Chilterns through the Blount family at Mapledurham, Martha Blount whom he loved being his 'scornful beauty', but Pope was no Chiltern man, or any real lover of country ways and life. There is no hint of the Chilterns in *Nightmare Abbey*, but it may have been written while Thomas Love Peacock was staying in the Chilterns. A forgotten writer, Frank Smedley, lived in Marlow and produced a highly enjoyable tale, *Frank Fairlegh* at the beginning of the nineteenth century. T. S. Eliot also lived in Marlow for a short while and perhaps it was while looking at the Oxfordshire ridge that he thought of 'the evening spread out against the sky like a patient etherised upon a table'. Jerome K. Jerome (*Three Men in a Boat*) is buried at Ewelme.

Probably no one reads *The Cloister and the Hearth* nowadays and certainly no one reads the less well-known but perhaps much better book, *Hard Cash*. But Charles Reade was once a best-selling writer and he lived and wrote in Ipsden, where the Chilterns open to flowing downland. The church there, with its strange north aisle, has already been mentioned, but outside it there is a curiosity of another kind, a cast-iron well head. This was the sort of work which in the '50s and '60s of last century foreshadowed the end of the village blacksmith. But no one could see it. Charles Kingsley, presumably also largely unread today, lived in the Chilterns for a while. But the inventor of 'muscular Christianity' was in no sense a Chiltern man.

With two exceptions the politicians kept out of the Chilterns until the gift of Lord Lee of Fareham gave the Prime Ministers of England the great house of Chequers Court as their permanent country home while in office. Burke was a true Chiltern man, however, living and dying in Beaconsfield, and Benjamin Disraeli, the first Lord Beaconsfield, drew all his life and work from his two Chiltern homes, Bradenham and his own house at Hughenden. His contemporaries thought of him as some kind of exotic Levantine, although he was born a Christian Englishman, his father Isaac, that true man of letters, being a convert from Judaism. All Disraeli's novels were conceived and written in the Chilterns, two of them, *Sybil* and *Coningsby*, most profoundly influencing English political thought and behaviour, and bringing home to the middle and upper classes of England the frightful separation of the English poor, as complete in those days as anything the Republic of South Africa or the Province of Ulster can show today between black and white or Protestant and Catholic. Not quite enough has been made by Disraeli's biographers about the Chiltern influences (in this one case, certain) which enabled a scholar recluse at Bradenham to foster one of the greatest of English Prime Ministers, a novelist, and the founder of modern Conservatism.

In modern times we have happily living and working in the Chilterns the poet and writer, J. H. B. Peel, the novelist P. H. Newby, the architects S. E. T. Cusdin at Little Gaddesden, and Ivan Smith at Ewelme, and, in addition to John Piper such painters as Judith Greenbury, Darlow and Priscilla Dimsdale. Journalists have always favoured the Chilterns largely because of nearness to London. 'Cassandra' of the *Daily Mirror*, Sir William Connor lived in Fingest, but that quiet spot could never have inspired so much powerful invective.

The nearness of Oxford has made the surrounding Chiltern villages havens for scholars, museum keepers, dons of every discipline and research students from all parts of the world. But these men and women are in the Chilterns for convenience, or under a more or less forced choice, and in the conditions of modern life the presence of a distinguished man of letters, a scholar, a great painter or world-famous biologist makes little difference to the life of a village. In a time of instant communication it is possible to live, without knowing it, next door to men who are shaking the world.

Finally a great explorer and a great naturalist live in the Chilterns. Lord Hunt the leader of the successful Everest expedition of 1953 lives at Aston near Henley, and Mr. Richard Fitter whose name is known wherever serious information is required about bird or beast lives above Chinnor, his wife being one of the acknowledged world authorities on rural conservation. The explorer and writer Col. Peter Fleming lived in his family home at Nettlebed until his death in 1971. His lovely actress wife, Miss Celia Johnson, survives him there.

It is a short enough list, this brief account of past and present notabilities in the Chilterns, but time will lengthen it. A million more people have come into the Chilterns since Waller wrote his beautiful lyrics just after the Civil War and among them, who can doubt it, must be some of the great figures of tomorrow.

CHAPTER TWELVE

Some Houses, Viewpoints and Enclaves

From the very nature of the country, and also from the somewhat poor quality of the farmlands in general, there are few great houses in the Chilterns and of these only a handful are open to the public. Among them, West Wycombe Park must be placed first, as a National Trust house of outstanding beauty and importance, and of easy accessibility. Close by is Bradenham Manor, worth a visit for its associations alone.

Pevsner calls Stoke House at Stoke Mandeville 'as good as any of its kind in the county'. But there is also Denham Place, the late Georgian mansion, Stoke Park at Stoke Poges, and Shardeloes. Hampden House may be seen, but not visited. There are two huge modern houses (less than 100 years old) in the Chilterns, Baron Rothschild's French château at Halton, now an R.A.F. Headquarters, and the Astor house, Cliveden near Burnham. The gardens here are the great attraction.

In looking through the various specialist books dealing with houses and gardens in the Chilterns, the visitor will be struck by the number of times the architect Wyatt (the 'destroyer') was called in for consultation or design and the frequent occurrence, in connection with the surrounding lands and gardens, of the names 'Capability Brown' and Repton. Both these men had a wonderful eye for the grouping of trees to achieve their compelling effect 50 to 100 years later. What a splendid gift that was, to plan quite literally for posterity. Even the greatest

16   *Spikelet on St. Mary's Church at Aylesbury*
17   *The 'Dutch' houses and Norman Tower of St. Mary's at Denham*

18 and 19 *High Wycombe and West Wycombe in 1940*

of the architects drew plans and elevations in the hope of seeing in brick, stone, and timber at least a part of their work. Brown and Repton landscaped in the mind, for our benefit now.

For many people it is the gardens and landscaped grounds of the great houses which make the warmest appeal. The interiors are all too often frozen into a fixed period of time, the owners seldom or never seen, their unlived-in great rooms and salons watched on fixed television by security guards, their treasures protected by ropes and compulsory routes. It is a sad experience to walk through any house which has been deadened into a museum and art gallery, and a refreshment of the spirit that nearly all the Chiltern beauty and attraction is out of doors and free. It is best to take the Chiltern houses as they occur on any chosen route, making an exception for West Wycombe Park, not least because it is a central point in a group of surpassing interest: West Wycombe village (also a National Trust property), the strange church on the hill, the Dashwood Mausoleum, the caves, and the lovely Chiltern views to be had from all about.

Chiltern viewpoints might well be an excursion in themselves. From every one of them may be gained the immediate knowledge that all is far indeed from being lost in England. In their order round the Chiltern map, beginning in Hertfordshire, the best of scores of look-out places might be, first, Little Gaddesden, Ivinghoe Beacon, and Wigginton. No one should visit Little Gaddesden church without giving himself the experience of the view behind it. Then come Coombe Hill outside Wendover with the possibility of sighting St. Paul's, and after that the view from the mound of Ellesborough church and Cymbeline's Mount. The ridge above Whiteleaf Cross has splendid views across the valley, as does the corresponding Bledlow Ridge. All the high ground from the tops of Wainhill, Chinnor Hill, Crowell Hill, and the fine line of the ridge all the way to the summit of Watlington Hill, give views of great magnificence out to Oxford and beyond.

Between Watlington and High Wycombe the country is too thickly wooded to allow outstanding viewpoints, but there is the memorable view, already mentioned, from the plateau by the church at the top of West Wycombe hill. On fine days all through the summer months the visitor may expect to share this view with great crowds of visitors. Over a thousand people a day go into the church between spring and autumn. Finally, completing the circle, there is a good view from the remains of the castle at Berkhamsted, and from the top of the Bridgewater Monument.

In driving to and from these points the motorist will be able to discover for himself the 'hidden Chilterns' and to learn at first hand the 'pulling away' power of the modern road systems. As a result of the great trunk motorways through the Chilterns there is now less traffic on the by- and secondary roads, with perhaps half a dozen exceptions, than at any time since the Middle Ages. To give a simple example, the road between the A40 at Stokenchurch and Aston Rowant is thick with traffic, setting about its business or returning from it, for half an hour or so each morning and evening. At all other times of the day this lovely road through the woods is almost entirely deserted. The motorist turning off the Chinnor or Princes Risborough road to Aylesbury at the signpost 'Great Missenden' will have steep, thickly wooded, and almost traffic-free roads all the way into the village itself. Because he comes immediately on to the Aylesbury/Wendover/Amersham trunk road towards London, there is at once the compulsion to drive on, not seeing the St. Christopher on the wall of Little Missenden church, or calling into the adult education centre of Missenden Abbey for permission to look at the superb parkland trees behind it.

These deserted traffic-free areas are quite easily picked out from the Chiltern Ordnance Survey Map. There is a five-mile circle around Checkendon of spectacular beauty at all times of the year, narrow roads and laneways twisting up hillsides and through the beechwoods. Reading and Oxford are less than ten miles away, but with a little trouble the motorist may have the day and the countryside almost entirely to himself. Not far away there is a similarly deserted tract at the top of the triangle made by the Nettlebed/Henley and Nettlebed/Reading roads. This is scarcely motoring country at all, and here is Dame Lys made famous by Mr. Peel's mention of an imaginary traveller sitting undisturbed across the Icknield Way from week-end to week-end.

One of the greatest and best of Chiltern solitudes is almost any· where inside the great circle (taking into account the small size of the Chiltern area as a whole, just 500 square miles), bounded by Henley, Marlow, Stokenchurch, Watlington, and Nettlebed. Here Wormsley is to be found, a marvellous wilderness, still untrodden by residents who have lived within five miles of it for generations. Here is Stonor Park and the great house of Lord Camoys, where the resident chaplain is an Archbishop of the Roman obedience. Here too are Fingest and Turville and Hambleden and all that densely wooded country which for hundreds of years harboured every type of hunted man and criminal from runaway serfs in Saxon times to the highwaymen of the late eighteenth century.

And in the very heart of the built-up Chilterns there is the 'lung' of Burnham Beeches, preserving the great pollarded trees which frightened Massingham, 'disturbing his spirit' when he came to them in the writing of his *Chiltern Country*. The whole area other than the enclosure of the trees is a dormitory, but in early spring or at any time in mid-week much of the feel of the original Chiltern countryside is preserved here. The roadways are asphalted, but the incredibly gnarled and twisted trees never fail of their appeal. All around, the Chilterns as such have ceased to exist, yet from Burnham Beeches to Beaconsfield and on to Oxford there are long stretches where the passing motorist will find himself running through wooded hills.

The great problem of description in the Chilterns is that of 'sameness'. From every Chiltern village and small town there is a view of rounded hills and beechwoods. Every steep hill is similar to every other steep hill, pitched at the same angle, shaded on both sides of the road by identical trees. That is of no consequence to the dedicated archaeologist or the inveterate church explorer, the fanatical photographer, botanist, or lover of sketching. There is enough to keep any of them happy and busy for a lifetime between Wendover and Watlington; enough ancient public houses to provide delightful interludes on any sightseeing tour; enough tea shops, and half a dozen first-class eating places, a large number for so small an area. What there is not is a show village like Bourton-on-the-Water or Burford; a great national centre of beauty like Bath; a dazzling cathedral. There is nothing to compare with the breathtaking East Anglian parish churches, or the cluster of great houses in the Dukeries. The American tourist on his way from London to Oxford will turn aside for Penn's grave at Jordans, but hardly (as he should), to read the plaque to Edmund Burke, that great upholder of American liberty, in the church at Beaconsfield. Ten years ago an American visitor, with our Civil War in mind, asked, at Chalgrove, if he was actually standing on the battlefield where Hampden was mortally wounded. 'Yes,' was the reply, 'but that was in oats at the time.' There is a lot of the Chilterns in that reply.

There is no 'tourist centre' in the Chilterns, most visitors regarding the area as 'getting out into the country' from London, or the Midlands. From their point of view it is perhaps a pity that the Chilterns have not contracted out of the twentieth century or that Wendover, say, has not been fixed forever at a point of time, an English Williamsburg. But ancient customs and ways, ancient monuments and old buildings are not destroyed by increases in population. Nearly everything which helped in the making of England is still to be found in the Chilterns, but sometimes, now, there needs to be a search. In the new sprawl of Chinnor there is still a High Street worth the short walk along its length, still an ancient church with some great treasures, still the Upper and Lower Icknield Ways, and still some of the most beautiful surrounding country in England. High Wycombe was called 'a devouring monster' in 1938 and it has more than doubled in population since then. But already, with the by-pass roads completed, its true character is again being revealed, and the point of Keene's Guildhall, for 30 years regarded as the cause of bottlenecks and traffic entanglements, is now once more clearly to be seen, putting a delightful finish to the wide High Street.

But over and over again in this book it has been stressed that the Chilterns are an area for the indulgence of whim. There is hardly a church without something to repay a brief visit, hardly a village without something to show of historical importance, hardly a road without a point of interest for almost every mile. 'This whole area is without a history,' said a famous Chiltern resident a year or so ago. Yet he was standing on a spot which must have taken the hoof imprint of Prince Rupert's horse, which has been a source of dispute between parish and county council since there were such things, where there is a right to get flint and a right to cut brushwood, where 600 feet up, sea fossils are to be gathered without prolonged search, and from which 600 years ago men set out armed with bill hooks and quarter staffs to fight for Sir John Oldcastle. He was standing at the entrance gate to his own property.

Enlargements

The Chilterns are full of places about which not enough has ever been said or written. In this book, for example, the Bedford monuments at Chenies have been mentioned but not described; there is a note about Latimer, but not the fact that visitors appear to go there mainly to watch traffic on the river, and are frequently disappointed. The Pendley Chapel at Aldbury is drawn to the reader's attention, but is not treated in depth.

It is painfully easy to bore the reader of guide- or descriptive books. In most cases he wants only bare indications; he can read a map as well as the author, he has access to as many libraries and books of general information. But nearly everyone, putting down a Chiltern book of the most general kind, will say 'Why is there so little about Stoke Poges, or High Wycombe, or Radnage, or ... ?' almost any well known or favourite spot. Others will be surprised at the omission of any account of Sir Joshua Reynold's visit to Burke, or the absence of reference to the distinguished poet, Miss Ruth Pitter. At a recent lecture in Ewelme, the first question asked of this writer was about a point deliberately left out of the lecture on grounds of lack of interest. At another Chiltern gathering the audience wanted more about the prevalence of the word 'End' in Chiltern village names, and perhaps rather less than they were offered about long forgotten habits of woodlanders and foresters. For one person interested in the beauty of West Wycombe Park there may be a hundred wanting to read about the Hellfire Club and the orgies, if any, in the Wycombe caves.

A rambling, supplementary chapter would seem to be an

answer, a mention of one point of interest perhaps leading to a brief discussion of another, 20 miles and hundreds of years away. This chapter, then, might be considered as an attempt to revive the old-fashioned discursive essay. Such an essay might prove to be the longest sequence in the book, having as the saying goes a little of everything for everybody, its order a steady progression through the book itself.

To make a start. There is much of interest in the prehistory of the Chilterns, as there so frequently is about all matters of speculation which cannot be proved. The unique population explosion in the village of Chinnor (there are now almost 5,000 people in a place where the population had, until ten years ago, remained constant since about the time of Domesday Book) has led to great interest in the *known* events of the past taking place there. The schoolchildren are aware that the first skirmish of the Civil War took place around the Church and in the High Street; they know that a Saxon skeleton was discovered in Church Lane within recent times, and that almost certainly a Saxon Church stood where St. Andrew's Church is now. But because the existing and widely known cement works was only opened in 1908 (and Portland cement itself was only invented towards the last quarter of last century), they are perhaps unaware that the Romans dug the chalk in Chinnor for their lime mortar, that the present church was built with it, or that a forgotten sea once washed it, or lay close by. Children from other towns are now brought to Chinnor to look for fossils in the chalk, or along the dreary wastes of surface-mined limestone. When those fossils were seashells man as we know him did not exist; but there are evidences of Iron Age man scattered fairly widely in the Chilterns. Traces of Bronze Age and the earlier ages of man are not so frequent, the harsh climate, worse then than now, would see to that.

As a preliminary to a brief discussion of such, almost modern, Chiltern history, Professor Coppock in his little book *The Chilterns* in the series, *British Landscapes Through Maps*, plunges his readers into a past so distant that the mind can scarcely grasp it.

He writes of an early Pleistocene Sea, the waves of which, he says, 'trimmed an Eocene peneplain'. And he brings that dimmest of visions into bold relief by setting out the names of present day settlements on the line of a forgotten Thames emptying into a vanished sea, Nuffield, Whipsnade, High Wycombe, Lane End, Stokenchurch, Maidenhead. The gravel beds which are now being surface-mined amidst so much controversy in the Chilterns of to-day, follow the gradients of an early Thames, and the ancestors, as Professor Coppock calls them, of rivers, not a river but rivers, which preceded, millions of years ago, the little Thame. With this in mind it is easier to grasp the fact that the steeper west- or south-facing slopes in the Chilterns are due to 'differential creep erosion', possibly the result of more frequent freeze-thaw during the glacial period. For all this region was under ice *after* the retreat of the Thames to roughly its present course.

The coming of man was an unimportant event in the Chilterns, and he first occurs in the Icknield Way loam belt and on the gravels between Mapledurham and Henley. But it has already been noted that the Romans, late as they were upon the scene, found a deserted countryside when they entered the Chilterns. They would have seen the Bronze Age barrows, almost contemporary with them, at Princes Risborough, and the Iron Age forts on Pulpit and Bodington Hills. But early man made little difference to the Chiltern landscape; it was left to present day man to do that. It was the West Saxons who first made any impact at all in the area, and after them we begin to know with some degree of certainty who came to what places, and why. By 1086 nearly all the settlements north-west of the Chilterns had come into being, but Professor Coppock reminds us that often two or more settlements were listed together. Domesday Book has only one Risborough, and Beaconsfield at that time was almost certainly counted as part of Burnham. After the settlements of mediaeval man, with some speculation, still unresolved about the place-names of those times, we know where we are. But what will distant space-roving men make of the remnants of present day Chinnor Glynswood, Naphill, and the new-planned outskirts of Thame?

20 *On the London/Oxford road at Beaconsfield: one of the four*
unspoiled ends
21 *Amersham High Street before the motor-car. Still one of the*
best small town walks in England

We have seen that the traditional industries of the Chilterns were, as they still are, based on the woodlands and the chalk. But there should be an additional word about Chiltern pillow lacemaking, a skill almost completely lost and yet remembered as a commonplace of the home by many old people still alive, and by all old people of 25 years ago. It is said that lacemaking was brought to Buckinghamshire and the Chilterns by Flemish makers escaping from the Spanish domination of the Low Countries. But it is also said that it was Catherine of Aragon who spread the cult from Ampthill, while she stayed there in 1531-33 during her appeal to the Pope about her divorce from Henry VIII. Certainly we are told that 'St. Catterns' day was always kept as a lacemakers' holiday in Buckinghamshire until the end of last century. The real centre of the industry was in north Buckinghamshire, clear of the Chilterns, at Newport Pagnell. In their *Little Guide to Buckinghamshire* Roscoe and Jowitt speak of 800 out of 1,275 inhabitants of Hanslope being engaged in lacemaking in 1901. At Marlow in the Chilterns, in 1626, Sir Henry Borlase founded and built a free school for 24 boys and 24 girls to 'knit, spin, and make bone lace'.

All the Buckinghamshire lace was pillow lace, and there were two kinds, bobbin and pillow point. By the end of the last century lacemaking was entirely a cottage industry, every village possessing many women familiar with the mysteries of the patterning derived from pins on paper round which the bobbins flew over a large lap-held pillow. Cowper described it all, as he observed it during his Olney years,

> *Yon Cottager who weaves at her own door*
> *Pillow and bobbins all her little store*
> *Content though mean, and cheerful if not gay*
> *Shuffling her threads about the livelong day*
> *Just earns a scanty pittance and at night*
> *Lies down secure her heart and pocket light*
> *She for her humble sphere by nature fit,*
> *Has little understanding, and no wit.*

22 *Harvesting near Princes Risborough 35 years ago. Stoocked corn and hand pitching have gone forever but the woodlands in the background are unchanged*
23 *The south front at Cliveden*

Cowper is out of fashion as a poet nowadays, but his verses are unmatched in depicting the submerged unknown condition of the English poor. Perhaps lacemaking went out because the cottager of humble sphere with little understanding and no wit had learned to read, and to take her place in a better world with a better social order. Whatever the reason lacemaking has gone from the Chilterns, and with the bobbins, the pins and the pillows have gone their strange but invariable ancillaries, the ducks. The former liking of country people everywhere for duck eggs as a breakfast delicacy has been killed by advancing knowledge about the diseases encouraged or actually caused by eating duck eggs; and the popularity of the bird itself as a seasonal delight with green peas has diminished with the rise of all-the-year-round vegetables and deep frozen food.

Nearly all the country pursuits of the last half century have waned in popularity, or gone altogether from the Chilterns. Every village still has its football team, as often nowadays a rugby team, but with the disappearance of the work-horse, the old slow ale-house games of the carter and the ploughman—skittles, dominoes, shove ha'penny—have gone too, or almost gone. Darts are still popular, but the players are a different breed and the game has a faster rhythm. The blacksmith has gone as well, other than as a plater of racehorses, or a shoer of ponies, and with him some of the children's toys. It is 20 years since any child skimmed a hoop in a Chiltern village, or, for that matter, whipped a top.

There are said to be only five long-straw thatchers in all the Buckinghamshire and Oxfordshire Chilterns, and in an age of universal 'combining' they have to have their straw grown specially for them, and to buy old reapers and binders whenever they can be found. There is plenty of work for them, but it is slow and unremunerative. With the virtual death of the art (reed thatching is on the increase and is profitable) has gone all the play toys and decorations made with straw. A corn dolly is a rare bird at Chiltern harvest festivals, and it is a sad sight to find dusty ten-year-old sheaves being brought out of store to help keep alive a pagan festival in Christian places of worship.

126

Fox-hunting and point-to-point racing are as popular as ever, the fields bigger than for many years, but covert shooting is changed indeed. The syndicated shoot is now a commonplace of the countryside and a farmer with a gun under his arm to shoot for his own pot an increasingly rare sight.

Only one of the ancient 'location sports' (such as the Olney pancake race) survives in the Chilterns, and that barely inside the area, the tug of war across the Thame at Tiddington. Old style country fairs are a thing of the past and, increasingly, there is pressure to stop the filling up of towns with all the fun of the fair under charter rights centuries old to the paralysing of motor traffic and the detriment of shop keepers. At certain times of the year it is impossible to move about in Princes Risborough, Amersham, or Thame. At those times there is a certain amount of Morris Dancing, no longer in these parts a serious country activity. No first class cricket is played anywhere in the Chilterns.

As anywhere where there is a sizable stretch of water, a vast increase in the use of the Thames for sailing and motor-boating has recently taken place, the Chiltern reaches being among the most popular. There is also much private boat activity on the Chiltern 'arms' of the canal system, about which this may be the place to say a little more.

The Grand Union comes into the Chilterns between Uxbridge and Gerrards Cross, making a winding passage through Watford to Berkhamsted to its highest point the Tring summit at Cow Roast. From there the canal passes between Aldbury and Tring to Bulbourne, the end of the summit level and the passage through the Chilterns. This is the place from which to *look down* the canal over the impressive seven Marsworth locks. Round about are Ivinghoe Beacon, the entrance to the Aylesbury Arm of the canal the twelfth-century church in Marsworth, and the famous church at Wing. There are also the Cheddington 'Saxon terraces' to be seen close by. Below Marsworth the country flattens and the Chilterns are left behind.

British Waterways have issued a booklet, in several parts, dealing with cruising on the Grand Union. Part 1 contains the whole

Chiltern section, and a short account of the almost insuperable difficulties faced and overcome in cutting it. The work took 12 years, including the construction of two long tunnels and the aqueduct at Wolverton. This collapsed in 1808 and the present Iron Trunk, one of the Buckinghamshire 'sights', dates from 1811. It is difficult to believe that the English canal system, so apparently outmoded nowadays as to be a serious financial burden, was regarded as a miracle of transport so recently as 1800 when scarcely a road in the country was fit for serious travel.

At Bridge 133 (bridges are numbered in the reverse direction from Braunston to London) the canal lies between the Upper and Lower Icknield Ways, described in the British Waterways booklet as two Roman roads, but as we have seen immeasurably older than that.

As we have seen, speculations about the origins of this Ancient Ridgeway, or Green Road as the Icknield Way has been called at different times are endless. These are particularly varied when the Way is considered on its route through the Chilterns as here it divides into Upper and Lower, the separation taking place in the middle of Dunstable where the Icknield Way cuts Watling Street, the Roman road to Holyhead, the prosaic A5 of modern maps. There are innumerable 'feeder tracks' into the Way all along its length from the East Anglian coast to Avebury in Wiltshire, and Stonehenge. For many years it was thought that Avebury was a centre for the performance of rites similar to those (still complete mysteries) which were said to take place in Eleusis. Recent excavations at Avebury have proved somewhat disappointing, but there is no doubt about the antiquities associated with the Icknield Way. Early Bronze Age man must have known it, helped to create parts of it, at least 1,800 years before the birth of Christ. The Upper Way, in the Chilterns, ran as high as man dared to walk above the water courses and springs, and it everywhere avoids the exposed summits of the ridges.

Throughout its history the Way has been used in the construction of contemporary roads. The Romans used parts of the

Lower Way through the Chilterns for their heavy transport, and parts of the Way are incorporated in our modern main roads. A stretch of the main Aylesbury/Tring road is formed from the Upper Icknield Way, and local names have been given to lengths of it, as in Wendover, where both Pound Street and High Street are parts of the Way, and in Chinnor where Lower Road runs first into Mill Lane and then into open country as a track. The Upper and Lower Ways unite near Watlington, cross Grims dyke (about which more must be said), as a single road, close to Nuffield, and leaves the Chilterns, on its way to Goring Gap, at Ipsden.

British Waterways are not alone in thinking of the Icknield Way as a Roman road; many of the people living on it or near it think the same, pointing as evidence to still clearly marked chariot ruts in some places, to a surviving breed of Roman snails, and to all the occupational remains to be found along the Way, such as the tumuli near Bledlow, and the site of a Roman private house at Terrick. But the Romans were simply users and improvers of the Way, just as the eighteenth-century roadmakers were, and as we are today. Before long Mill Lane, in Chinnor, will be widened and improved to carry heavy traffic away from the village. This will modify some of the existing Lower Icknield Way.

Our pit-dwelling forefathers in the Chilterns chose to live along the Upper Way, which has several of their 'complexes' still. People living now at Ellesborough, at Lodge Hill above Princes Risborough, and high above Chinnor on the county boundary between Oxfordshire and Buckinghamshire may reflect that their gardens knew the foot of man 5,000 years ago.

Oddly enough the main object of controversy in discussions about the antiquities of the Chilterns is not the Icknield Way at all, but a much more recent construction, the Grimsditch, or Dyke. Massingham, as we have seen, called it 'the longest serpent of antiquity', but it was made hundreds of years after the last Roman left Britain.

The antiquarian O. G. S. Crawford thought it was a tribal boundary or a fortification marking the separation of kingdoms, and

Pevsner thinks that the Saxons dug it to mark the eastern boundary of Cuthwulf's territory sometime after his capture of Aylesbury in 571 or thereabouts. We know so little of our own Dark Ages, or our early Kings, about whom we confidently tell our children stories dealing with the burning of cakes, oaths on tombs, meetings on bridges or payments to Danes. Hardly any of the men taking an actual part in the early events of our history could read or write, and we have no reason to suppose that the reporters of those days, mostly enclosed monks, were any more accurate than the average newspaperman of today.

J. H. B. Peel thinks that the Ditch may have been constructed by native Britons as a defence against the Danes, but this seems unlikely as at no point along its route is any escarpment of the Chilterns commanded. On the contrary the Ditch clings always to the valleys, hugging the woods. It could not possibly provide a rallying shelter against an invading force which could have occupied all the heights above it, or overrun it, at a score of points.

Annan Dickson thinks the Ditch might be an elaborate obstacle contrived for the prevention of cattle raiding. It is true enough that from the earliest recorded times, and right up to the highwaymen of the eighteenth century, the Chilterns were the home of lawless and desperate men, and that eyes might have been fastened on the stock in the Vale of Aylesbury. But the stock would not have been of special value, as they are today. There were no pastures in the Vale, or anywhere else in England, capable of fattening livestock, for hundreds of years after the building of the Ditch. When in the nineteenth century Peacock wrote of 'the valley sheep being fatter', he really meant bigger; the sciences of stock and grass improvement at the date of his poem were both in their infancy. Annan Dickson does not overlook the reasonable possibility that the Ditch may have been intended to protect and define grazing rights along its length, but, as he himself points out, a few marker posts would have served that purpose equally well.

Several writers, including Alison Uttley in her book on Buckinghamshire, suggest that the Ditch is prehistoric, but this it most certainly is not. Nowhere in the world has prehistoric man left any greater memorial of his presence than a few shards, or some faint indications that he had lighted a fire. Now and again his stone or flint weapons are found, or the remnants of a near fossilised skeleton. A great undulating geographical feature like the Ditch would have been entirely beyond his dawning intelligence and constructional abilities.

In the end, and remembering always the strange appearance of the Ditch through Nettlebed Woods, as Highmoor Trench, which is entirely out of its general character, the Ditch may safely be regarded as a Boundary of Kingdoms, but by no means of tribes. No early British tribe commanded the means of constructing so great an artifact. As a frontier between Mercia, Wessex, and perhaps some of Northumbria, put there by the agreement of emerging kings, or left-over powerful regional chiefs, the whole great earthwork makes sense, including its very route, along all the easy places. The great men of the time could have stood on either side of it, bargaining for a curve here, a long bend there, just as it is today. Only such men could have organised and set to work the thousands of impressed serfs who would clearly have been needed. On a summer's evening, standing anywhere along the Ditch and allowing the imagination to riot, it is almost possible to see these labouring hordes as they and their masters set about the establishment of a mystery for posterity.

Not enough has been said in this book about the great Royal Forests which so greatly influenced the whole life of the Chilterns in Norman times. These paradoxically hedged about, as it were, the already densely wooded Chilterns, thus perpetuating the sparseness of settlement. We have already noted the complete disappearance of Bernwood, the Royal Forest lying all round Oakley and Brill. Most of Windsor Royal Forest has also gone, but the settlements of eastern Berkshire are still affected by it. In practice the Normans 'cleared' their way into the Chilterns, keeping to the main valleys and leaving the wooded uplands alone wherever they could. In those times there was far more of the open Chiltern Heaths than there is today and, undoubtedly some of the commonage grazing took place actually in the woodlands. But the pressure of the Royal Forests helped to create the Chilterns as we know them; and the fearful penalties for taking game in the forests helped to make the deeper Chilterns the natural home of outlaws.

In the earlier part of this work a little was said about most of the Chiltern towns, but all of them have a peculiar charm which can only be savoured by walking about in them. Pevsner dignifies this process by his delightful use of the word 'perambulation', and it is just the leisurely movement implied by the word which is required. What motorist proceeding along the A40 towards Oxford and passing the point 'Denham' has any conception of the delights awaiting him a few hundred yards from that highway? There is still an unspoiled and altogether delightful old-world village of Denham, a single street of beautiful houses with a fourteenth-century church. In the church is one of only two brasses in all England to an Abbess, Dame Agnes Jordan of Sion who died in 1544. There is also a Last Judgement, or Doom as it is known here. King Charles II hid in Denham, they say, after the Battle of Worcester, probably in Denham Court. There are huge building developments all about, and the great film studios are still there across the main road. But the village itself would be recognised by Dryden if he came here again to see his friend Sir William Bowyer in 'the most delicious garden in England'.

Another Chiltern town, almost always overlooked by motorists, is Watlington, since it is possible to drive through it without even suspecting the presence of the parallel High Street. It is one of the most charming of the little Oxfordshire towns, and it is a rare pleasure to discover, in the shops, the post office and 'the local', that the England of the warm welcomes so often described as disappearing or indeed as gone for ever is still flourishing in Watlington, as in reality it must be in hundreds of towns and villages throughout the country. Certainly that is still the case in Great Missenden, in Wendover, in Princes Risborough, High Wycombe, Amersham, and even Tring. But the true atmosphere of any town and its people cannot be sensed from a motor-car.

There is a word which, in the Chilterns, might be added to the 'perambulation' of Pevsner; it is 'serendipity', 'the faculty of making happy and unexpected discoveries by accident'. The Chiltern towns are full of opportunity.

As are the fields and hedgerows. Nothing has, so far, been said about the botany of the Chilterns, because the taste for identifying the wild flowers of the countryside seems to have altered. Fifty years ago along every English lane in summertime men and women with vasculum cases, the long tin box with carrying strap used by all botanists for collecting specimens, were a commonplace. Now, and despite the spectacular success of Keble Martin's *Concise British Flora*, the amateur botanist is a rare sight. Yet there is much for him in the Chilterns. Obviously lists of plants which may be found are out of place in a book of this kind but it should be mentioned that there are one or two of the rarer Orchises in the Chilterns, one so rare that its locale is a closely guarded secret. All the commoner plants are in great abundance in the area, but some rarities are to be found in the woodlands, notably a bramble, *Rubus hirtus, var. flaccidifolius*. There is still some Lily of the Valley to be found in Chiltern woods. On the chalk there are all the expected plants and a rare *Carex C. Paradoxa*, has been noted in a chalk meadow by the Chess, not far from Chenies.

Because of the wonderful omnipresence of the beech tree there is in all the Chiltern books a tendency not so much to minimise as to omit altogether mention of the large quantities of other beautiful trees all over the area. On woodland borders the crabapple is common, and lovely in spring. Some of the finest elms in the country are to be found in the Chilterns and the more pronounced chalklands have much yew and holly. There is said to be native box at Ellesborough, but this has not been seen. There are many glorious specimen hornbeams everywhere on the chalk and the river trees are of course plentiful, many varieties of willow and much alder. There is also a great deal of fine ash. The oak is not too common in the Chilterns though plentiful enough just north of the main ridges.

The wild animals of the Chilterns lie ever closer as the human population thickens: they know that man is the greatest of the predators. It is 15 years since a fox barked on the outskirts of Chinnor, and longer since a badger crept off the hill nearly to the Post Office, but both species are not far away. There are deer everywhere in the Chilterns and they may be seen quite frequently in the quiet places. It is probably still true to write of the Chilterns that the whole picture of the fauna is similar to that of all the Southern and Midland counties. This is also true of the birds, although it is less likely than once it was that the nightingale haunts the Chilterns in great abundance, filling every copse with song. There is a unique warbler (alas, not seen), in the close preserve of Chinnor Hill, the top of which is now safe for ever with the Oxfordshire, Buckinghamshire and Berkshire Natural History Society. The pastime of bird-watching has never been so popular as it is now and all over the Chilterns there are great opportunities for indulging in it. There are not so many places in England where nearly all the woodland, meadow and garden birds may be observed in the course of a short walk. And there is always the chance of a surprise.

The impact of television has produced a host of amateur antiquarians, as the patient rubbers of church brasses demonstrate. They are active, too, with cameras, although men and women with sketch blocks or easels are no longer a common sight. It is remarked in the Bibliography that Peel's *Discovering the Chilterns* contains two or three pages on 'How to Look at a Church'. These simple notes double the pleasure always obtained on wandering into a Chiltern church, particularly as most of them are not particularly rich in spectacular treasures. A sense of knowledgeable power comes over a church-visitor who reading in the local guide about a rare and beautiful misericord in the parish church knows, from Mr. Peel, that he must look for it on the underside of a hinged choir seat; or that 'crocketing' refers to the decoration on the sides of steeples, and must be viewed from outside.

It is important to look closely at simple objects in Chiltern churches as there are no 'great' churches anywhere in the area Even Ewelme has nothing to show comparable with, say, the roof angels at Blythburgh; and the Bedford monuments in the parish church at Chenies are shut off from the visitor, as are not the splendid de la Pole memorials in the church at Wingfield, in Suffolk. But in nearly every Chiltern church there is something to take the eye or appeal to the spirit, and it is often important to check that an ugly mid-Victorian restoration *outside*, conceals (as in the case of the Bradshawe memorial in Wendover), something entirely unique and beautiful within.

The restorers of the mid-nineteenth century did irreparable damage to many Chiltern churches, while simultaneously neglecting and allowing to fall into complete decay numerous buildings worthy of their attention. It is important to remember, however, that the restorers, like ourselves, were men of their time, and that tastes change markedly with every generation. It is impossible to commend much of their work: the spreading of concrete over mediaeval treasures, the throwing out of ancient pulpits, fonts, church furniture, the tiling of floors, the provision of pitch-pine benches. But in their day the churches had nearly all been left uncared for and crumbling, heaps of rubble left about in the aisles for years on end, pillars and arches fortunate to be coated only with thick whitewash. The parochial councils and wealthy residents or patrons who took these churches in hand were not faced as we are today with the simple dangers of subsidence, mouldering stonework, weakening bell-towers, overcrowded graveyards. They found themselves called upon to repair and restore ruins in many of which three or four services a year were often the sole connections with a tradition of Christian worship. In 1863 the rubble in Chinnor parish church was window high, and the contemporary report of Francis Buttanshaw speaks of pews 'in every degree of dirt and dilapidation'. Strong ruthless measures were needed and if sometimes they were too strong, at least the buildings were cleaned, and in an age when nearly everyone went to church, places were provided in which they could at least sit down. Cromwell's men did more damage in the Chilterns than any of the restorers of the 1860s.

In the already mentioned *Little Guide to Buckinghamshire*, there are about five pages dealing with (mostly Chiltern) monastic remains, churches, notable brasses, fonts, communion tables and the like. And everything listed has survived the hands of various restorers. There will come a time when the Italianate church at West Wycombe will require, let us say, extensive rebuilding. It is not at all likely that the restorers of that distant time will set about recreating what stands there now. Already, to take a more prosaic example, Scott's tower and spire at Princes Risborough, dating only from 1907, have an old-fashioned rather than a properly 'architectural' look, and the casual visitor might not be drawn, thereby, into a church known to have been almost completely rebuilt and restored in the 1860s. But that visitor would miss the superbly exciting Early English window in the south aisle, deeply recessed and with two rows of pillars. There is something unexpected like that in nearly every Chiltern church.

There are unexpected secular buildings, too. It has already been remarked that only a handful of the great Chiltern houses could be considered as in the front rank, but some of the smaller town houses are of singular beauty, as are some of the High Streets in which they stand, Old Amersham for example or Thame. Everywhere there are cottages and small dwelling houses worth at least a passing glance and the thought that although now they may be surrounded by estate bungalows or worse, they have outlasted many reigns and governments, and will certainly outlast much of the rubbish which overshadows them.

It has been said that the Buckinghamshire Chiltern country is the epitome of England, and in many ways that is true. Soon it will be more true than ever. There was a time when a Devonshire lane, a stretch of Yorkshire moor, a Kentish hopfield or orchard were said to reflect all that England meant and was. Times have changed with the rise of the motor-car and the construction of the great trunk roads. Nowadays England is evoked for most of us by an old cottage standing at the roadside, a clatter of children on horseback, a motor-car at the edge of a beechwood, a small hill against the sky. All these things are to be found in Buckingham-shire, less than 40 miles from central London. The Devonshire lane is becoming a hindrance to communication, the moorlands are no longer mysterious and deserted, the hopfields are dwindling and worked by machinery, a modern commercial orchard needs the constant attention of a skilled chemist.

The Chilterns are cut from east to west by the usual great roads, now a commonplace of travel. But from north to south it is not so easy to get about and a man must pick his way. High Wycombe is now less than an hour by car from London, but there is no direct road for a similar mileage northwards, and such a journey will still take twice as long.

Motoring can once again actually be enjoyable in the Chilterns, made so precisely by those great by-passes and trunk systems which have been so bitterly opposed as the various plans for them became known. The traffic upon them always seems to an ob-server to be going nowhere at ever greater speeds, but, as an im-mediate example, any turning to left or right off the A40 between Denham, where it enters the Chilterns and the approaches to Oxford where it leaves them, leads directly to peace and quiet. When after 20 years of controversy the final extensions through the Chilterns of the M4 feeder systems (whether on the original Whitehall plan or on the better but recently again rejected Arup/ Jellicoe Route) are brought to a conclusion the effects on traffic will be very great. The children now growing up will not care which route was selected, but a number of villages will again have to be sought along quiet, almost lonely, roads. That must surely prove a blessing in the long run.

CHAPTER FOURTEEN

The Future in the Chilterns

No prophet is ever entirely right, and from Old Mother Shipton onwards most of the prophets of English Doom have been decidedly wrong. It is so easy to deduce from the petty circumstances of a particular time and place that all is lost for ever. And so it is, that here in the Chilterns, every new development, every shift in the growth pattern of a village, any suggestion that a factory might be placed here or there, produces feelings of deepest gloom, particularly among those local inhabitants most nearly affected.

It is inevitable that this should be so since all the experts are agreed that the southern escarpment of the Chiltern Hills is destroyed for ever, and that more and more expansions from London must occur. The main questions now are first what *should* be saved and then what *can*.

It is customary for the members of conservation societies to regard the modern planner as an enemy. This may be wrong; the planner thinks of himself primarily as a conservationist, weighing the needs of people against those of animals, botanical specimens, and that vague abstraction 'the environment'. It is with that defence, 'the needs of people', that planners drive roads through beautiful countrysides, turn villages into townships, disturb water tables by flooding valleys, put a thousand identical houses into a rural setting to produce a New Town. There will be more supporters for such policies than opponents, many more.

Many thousands of them have managed to escape from a stunted town life into the air of the Chilterns simply because houses have been made available to them. They will of course be the protesters of tomorrow, some of them are protesting against further development already, but that is understandable. What all of us in the Chilterns of today should be thinking about, however, is the decisive period of the next 20 years. The problems of ordinary day-to-day living which have been raised by the housing explosion in the Chilterns are enormous, and there is no evidence anywhere that they are being taken seriously. Some of them are not even recognised, certainly never discussed.

On the surface the main difficulties affecting life in the present-day Chilterns are those of education, shopping facilities, transportation, and community living. These are not insuperable, although it can only be a matter of a few years, certainly not more than a decade before a great many little children are not going to receive the education, even the simple schooling, which their young parents had. There are not going to be enough school places, or enough teachers to deal with the hordes of babies already with us. Nevertheless something is being done; a few new schools are being built and a few old ones converted. Nearly every village hall or meeting place in the Chiltern settlements is already being used as a classroom for some part of the day. The 'temporary' classroom unit is now a commonplace, little hutments scattered about the surroundings of the actual school. The conception of the highly qualified teacher has had to be abandoned in the remoter areas, school managers being happy to secure the services of reasonably trained men and women who actually love children, have patience with them, and can read and write. That is almost enough in any case, and it will have to serve for a long time.

Shopping facilities are becoming increasingly difficult. This is the age of branded goods supplied from central depots to fill demands estimated by computer. The choice of goods in outlying districts becomes more limited every day, with the result that the shopper is driven for her requirements into neighbouring small towns. This raises the whole question of country transportation.

Practically every man in the Chilterns above the simplest kind of general labourer needs or appears to need a motor-car to reach his work, and the filling of this need has driven country public transport almost off the roads. If the worker lives on an estate, built on the outskirts of a Chiltern village, as they nearly all are, his driving off to work leaves the wife, mother, or housekeeper, marooned. It is thus common to find 'two car families', as those in high income brackets used to be called, on all the estate developments. The women are housebound if there is no second car, or condemned to walks of well over a mile each way for their ordinary day-to-day requirements.

Community living imposes severe tensions. Most of the new Chiltern dwellers reached adult life in big cities or giant London or Midland suburbs and it is difficult for them to become accustomed to some of the quite trifling but age-old accompaniments of country life. As an example one of the commonest features in the correspondence columns of local papers are complaints about bonfires. The modern estate garden presents no problems of hedge-clipping disposal, and the bonfires of old-established cottagers are said to damage washing, deposit dirt on windows and furniture, and prevent the use of gardens as sitting-out places. In time old residents will have to give way to these demands. They are already greatly outnumbered.

It is surprising to hear or to read about the new types of complaint at parish meetings. Dustbins set out for collection are highly dangerous; the village sidewalks, as, alas, pavements are now all too generally called, too narrow for the passage of prams; there are no public lavatories. People are no longer prepared to walk if it is possible for them to drive. There are thus frequent requests for more and more parking facilities in villages which until the middle 'fifties could handle all the traffic likely to visit them.

It has already been mentioned in this book that the Chilterns are one of the birthplaces of that English characteristic, 'reserve'. For centuries people here have 'put up' with their situation, happily doing without street-lighting or any of the rest of the so-called amenities. All that is coming to an end. The new Chiltern resident gets up at meetings and speaks his mind freely, and his wife is not backward in standing to support him. It is a commonplace to read of parish clergy being contradicted in public, an unthinkable state of affairs less than 20 years ago. Times have changed, and manners and customs with them.

But despite all this the Chiltern country has not changed and the effect of these little hills on newcomers is very real. There is scarcely a village in Oxfordshire and Buckinghamshire without a local branch of the C.P.R.E, or its own local society affiliated to that body. There is a difference between the outlook of dwellers on the new Chiltern estates and of those on the great settlements in the commuter belts of Surrey and Kent which look to London for culture and entertainment as well as for work. When all is said and done the main topic in the Chilterns among all the thousands of new young mortgage holders is 'a better life for the children'. That is a worthy ambition indeed, and it is here among the hills and beechwoods that it can be fulfilled. There are certain to be further despoliations within the next decade, but if each extension is challenged and no brick laid until the whole plan has been considered in all its bearings, then the Chilterns as we know them today will survive in all their beauty. For it cannot be too strongly emphasised that despite all the ravages of the past and much of the purely selfish money-grabbing extensions of the last few years, the new Chiltern settlements are really and truly 'in the country'. There is not one of them, beyond Beaconsfield, from which solitude and deep countryside cannot be reached in a walk of a quarter of an hour. Perhaps, as the pessimists are never tired of saying, there will come a time when all the Chiltern country is absorbed in London, as most of the southern escarpment is now. Maybe, but when that happens the last reader of these pages will have been dead for a hundred years or more. Let us enjoy this lovely countryside while it is still with us.

CHAPTER FIFTEEN

A Last Look Round

There is no part of the Chilterns completely unknown to this writer and, as he takes his leave, he feels constrained to set out a few more general thoughts, to suggest a few more places worth a visit, and to try and recapture something of the essence of a countryside of which those who live in it never tire, and which has exercised a personal spell over him for more than 20 years.

It is not really true as the jargon of present times has it that 'places are people', but neither is it true that the Chilterns could, or ever did exist in a vacuum. Only deserts can do that, and no longer deserts if there be oil beneath them. One of the finest and most deserted walking areas in the whole Chiltern country, the Amersham, Great Missenden, High Wycombe triangle, is in reality teeming with people. But once clear of those three main terminal points every square mile is peaceful and, in spring, unmatched in England. It is not, of course, what is known as 'serious' walking country, but there is little to compete with it for pleasure within a 50-mile radius of London. All footpaths are, as we have seen, clearly marked and the intersecting roads themselves are comfortably free from thick traffic and fast drivers. One can stroll.

There is a short motor-drive in the Chilterns, easily reached from London or the Midlands, which should be taken whenever an overseas visitor wishes to be shown what he will call the 'Real England'. All of England is that, but visitors from abroad have an image in their minds and there is no need to disappoint them.

All that is necessary to enchant the visitor is to turn left off the A40 from London to Oxford a mile beyond the great Stokenchurch roundabout. Immediately there are five miles of Chiltern country, the starting places of a maze of footpaths, and, to help in the work of preservation, half a dozen picnic points. At the radio station for Christmas Common, turn right for the summit of Watlington Hill with, on a fine day, its stupendous views to Oxford or the Vale of Aylesbury, then back to the London road via Watlington itself, and the now said to be 'doomed' village of Lewknor. At the turn for London is the Lambert Arms a meeting place for the area.

Something, but not enough, has already been said about the countryside around Fawley. Although it is easily reached from either Henley or Watlington it is so guarded with hills and narrow lanes that there is seldom any serious traffic. The whole area is the epitome of the Oxfordshire Chilterns and there is so much within easy reach of it, Stonor Park, Fingest, Turville, the Thames itself. Five miles away is Nettlebed, a starting point for the whole Oxfordshire ridge.

It has been said earlier that many of the Chiltern place names are comparatively recent, mediaeval rather than Saxon; some of them as late as the fourteenth century. They are not the less beautiful for that: Ellesborough, Princes Risborough, Great Hampden, Little Missenden, Amersham, High Wycombe, Checkendon, Woodcote, Rotherfield Greys, The City. The woods and smaller hills have names even more evocative: Withy Copse, Nippers Grove, Highmoor, Benhams, Great Wood, Pheasants Hill, Whiteleaf Cross, Sprigg's Alley. All the churches look back to the ages of faith; they are named after Apostles St. Mary Magdalene, All Saints, Holy Cross, and St. Nicolas. English devotion to St. Christopher did not begin with the motor-car and will outlive his banishment by Rome. There is no church of St. Christopher in the Chilterns, but the several wall paintings of him have been noticed.

There are five pages of 'Artists' in the index of Pevsner's little book on the buildings of Buckinghamshire, mostly of the great builders and decorators, and of the landscape gardeners. Many of them worked in the Chilterns, Robert Adam is there and 'Capability' Brown. Flaxman is there too, represented by an unimportant memorial in the church at Slough. Henry Keene is well represented in High Wycombe, so is Nollekens, who has two examples of his work in West Wycombe church. The Roman Catholic church in Marlow has much work by Pugin. James Wyatt came often to the Chilterns and the girls' school, Wycombe Abbey, is largely his. But the absence or fleeting appearances with minor examples of the truly great house-builders and architects in the Chilterns proper reflects the harsh nature of the country from the point of view of those desiring vast houses dominating rich estates. This is not the place for them, nor are there the superb local stones of the Cotswolds, of Bath and its surroundings, or of the Dukeries. Limestone is not the happiest of materials from which to build a dry house. It 'weeps', as the builders say.

There is another aspect of the Chilterns which should be considered. Descriptive attempts are to some extent hampered from the first day of researches by the fact that the area, though small and homogenous, is yet concerned to a greater or less degree with the affairs and boundaries of five English counties. Some writers have overcome this by confining their Chiltern observations to Buckinghamshire about which there is an immense literature. Others have picked a few plums in the hidden parishes and villages of Chiltern Oxfordshire. Massingham, when he came to Hertfordshire, merely put a few paragraphs under the heading 'Happy homely Hertfordshire' in his section dealing with what he called 'Conquered Country'. Anyone writing today of the Berkshire Chiltern heaths finds himself mainly concerned with the outskirts of Reading, a daunting prospect.

Yet the task has had to be faced. Little Gaddesden is every bit as much a Chiltern village as Ewelme, some would say with a more definite claim. The Chalfonts and Berkhamsted cannot be left out merely because their character has changed; and, indeed it is by no means certain that any place is destroyed beyond redemption by the mere addition of buildings. Graham Greene, recently on pilgrimage to his Berkhamsted birthplace, has revealed that the lane and 'hiding place' he used, clear of the town, as a schoolboy 50 years ago, are still there and still exactly as he remembered them. It is as absurd to dismiss Burnham Beeches because it is now almost part of London, and is indeed owned by the City of London, as it would be to leave out High Wycombe because it is now three times bigger than it was 25 years ago.

The treasures in all the Chiltern places are mostly safe, but now they must be sought. And it must be easier to take a County map, and plan routes and excursions about it, than to look at sheet 159 of the Ordnance Survey, 'The Chilterns', with the frightening task of making a start, and of carrying a reader over so varied a territory, made into one piece by the accident of hills and woodlands.

It is tempting to stray over the Chiltern boundaries for it is not possible to live in the Oxfordshire Chilterns without some familiarity with much on their fringes. There is Thame, of which a great deal could be said in an Oxfordshire book, but little more than a mention in a Chiltern book. There are Brill and Long Crendon, there is the festival village of Towersey, in plain and full view of the hills but not of them. There is Chalgrove and the Civil War battle of 1643. The list could be extended all round the map.

Another difficulty in guide-book writing is the beauty of the Chilterns. One can sit all day on top of Watlington Hill, or on the outskirts of Checkendon. But what is there to say about those places that a visit of one minute will not make plain?

A few months ago this writer was handed a small book about a small village in Dorset. There was a map, there were two or three pictures, there were less than a hundred pages of text. The book represented a full day's work every day for ten years. It is by that kind of devoted labour alone that the Victoria County Histories of England have been produced, or for that matter the history of any place in the Chilterns. What for example happened in many of the Thames Valley churches between about, say, the 1780s and the accession of Queen Victoria? What was it like to be poor then and living in Turville? The researcher finds quite often that for that half century or so there are no true records, that he is dealing with a forgotten age, that literally and truly nobody knows. All history is but an attempt to write down what is known to have occurred. But the writing down is coloured by the religious and political bias of the historian and all too often those writings are destroyed by dissenting or careless successors. Every schoolboy knows about the plucking of red and white roses to begin our Civil War. How dull that the bloody struggle actually began as a scrimmage before lunch in a St. Albans garden on 22 May 1455. And that of course it was not 22 May as we know it, but well into our present-day June. That is why there were roses to pick. This book has quoted Professor Coppock making his way with certainty along the shores of a forgotten sea washing against the limestone cliffs of Lane End between High Wycombe and Marlow. Not even Professor Coppock could name the crusader in Chinnor Church, or give us a positive fact about King Cymbeline, or state with conviction that William the Conqueror really spent a night in Bledlow. The railway line from Watlington to Princes Risborough has now been closed for about 15 years. How many of those who used it every day for years can still name without pausing the stations and halts along its way?

So a Chiltern book can only skim and pick. It would take a dozen years to write a full account of Chiltern forestry, of Chiltern furniture, of the Icknield Way in the Chilterns, of the Grimsditch. One would have wished to devote whole chapters to the digging of the Grand Union Canal and its Chiltern branches, 'arms' as they were called. The Reverend A. J. Foster wrote an entire book about the Chiltern Hundreds, and another could quite easily be made from accounts of the Lollards and their wild preachings in the Chiltern towns and villages. A year or so ago the tradesmen of Thame produced a leaflet, 'An Hour in Thame'. That is the measure of today's interest; a serious book about Thame would take a lifetime and still be incomplete.

Every church in the Chilterns has a booklet, leaflet, or set of notes about it displayed in the porch. Some are minor historical studies of importance, others draw attention to the font and pulpit and are done. All of them are the result of much labour and of delvings into parochial records, in themselves prepared through the centuries at the whim of and with all the personal prejudices of incumbents. For 200 years, and perhaps still, it was more important for parish records to number the village Papists and Dissenters, and to list annual Communions, than to record the crumbling of a Saxon arch or the filling of an aisle with rubbish. But who wants to know of all this, now, apart from devoted archaeologists and antiquarians?

Perhaps it is enough to drive about in the Chilterns, or to picnic on the edge of Shirburn Wood, or to sit outside Little Gaddesden church looking at our great heritage, or to stand on West Wycombe Hill discovering that all is not yet lost. Perhaps it is enough to look through the glass in Chenies church, reflecting on the Bedford Monuments, or to be glad that certain hideous restorations were made in many places and thus a church preserved. Perhaps it no longer matters that the Cook memorial is hidden away by the National Coal Board, or that hypermarkets in deep country are soon to take the place of old-fashioned supermarkets in the towns. Taste is still a matter of education, buildings will still crumble if not restored, paintings fade into nothingness, as on the walls at Little Kimble.

But on 20 September 1971, there was not a soul with whom to share Christmas Common and the summit of Watlington Hill had only two other visitors. There were only five motor-cars seen in the whole lovely stretch from the little town itself, up over the hill, past the mysterious chalk 'wedge', and down through woods about to put on the red and gold of autumn to the Oxford/London road. That is what the Chilterns are about, and the lifetime of three oaks, the limits of the oldest families, will not exhaust their glory.

CHAPTER SIXTEEN

Some Afterthoughts

Thirty years of Chiltern experience is more than enough to provide memories for the rest of a lifetime. Everything has changed, most of it for the better, and the next decade may well see reversions to a past many think has gone for ever. There is little doubt now that world supplies of crude oil are running out fast and that the mainly hideous pattern of life imposed on all of us by the private motor-car will shortly be disturbed. Some expert opinion holds that private motoring may have to be officially banned before the mid-eighties of this century (less than 15 years from now) and that waterways may once more be called upon for the transportation of heavy traffic. It is likely that by the turn of this century the reign of the internal combustion engine will be over, and the motor-car, as we know it, relegated to museums with the stage-coach. Many readers of this chapter will live to see the changes foreshadowed here; may even see the return of the steam locomotive.

The Chiltern people will take everything as they have always done, letting the tides flow over them and recede. Apart from the new bustling communities all life is slow hereabouts, men and women live a long time, preferring to look backwards rather than towards the political dawns which they have been promised from one source or another for generations.

In 1782 a German pastor, Carl Philipp Moritz, walking through the Chilterns towards Oxford, found himself in Nettlebed. He had tried to stay at one or two country inns on the boundaries of Henley but the owners would not take him in, and Henley itself he had felt to be 'too grand'. England then was not much of a

place for 'foreigners', and it has been remarked earlier in this book that at the end of the eighteenth century the whole Chiltern country was harsh and sparsely populated. So Pastor Moritz walked on to Nettlebed. He loved it. He was made welcome at the Inn, it must have been the White Hart, and was set down to a meal with some soldiers and the servants.

He had a lesson at once in English class distinctions as a post-chaise drew up while his meal was going on and 'in a moment ... the whole house was set in motion in order to receive with all due respect these guests who no doubt were supposed to be persons of consequence'. In fact the post-chaise had stopped for its two passengers to have a pint of beer apiece, but 'the people of the house behaved to them with all possible attention for they came in a post-chaise'.

The next day, when Pastor Moritz had put on some clean clothes he became a parlour guest and was called 'Sir' by every-one. And he went to church, finding our Church of England service strange indeed, but much to his taste, above all the congregational singing of the Forty-Seventh psalm. Special musical instruments were employed at this point perhaps to give point to 'God is gone up with a merry noise; and the Lord with the sound of the trump'. He thought it was all lovely, performed 'by the peaceful and pious inhabitants of this sweet village'.

This Chiltern visitor was unable to speak very highly of the sermon or of the incumbent. He thought him unprepossessing and 'a little distant and reserved; and I did not quite like his returning the bows of the farmers with a very formal nod'. What he did like were the tombstone inscriptions and what he called 'the orderly and good people'. He could hardly tear himself away. 'Three times did I get off in order to go on further and as often returned, more than half resolved to spend a week or more in my favourite Nettlebed'. He had found himself 'so perfectly at home'.

As he would today. The reader of this little work will recall that some of the most beautiful country in all England lies be-tween Nettlebed and Henley, and the Forty-Seventh Psalm can no doubt still be heard there as occasion offers. Unhappily the old

English custom of playing on individual musical instruments at services in English churches seems to have died out everywhere.

Less than 150 years later another visitor walked through much the same part of England, and he too, wrote down his experiences. The walker was Edward Thomas, the Welsh poet, so soon to be killed in the 1914-18 War. He had a different vision from that of Pastor Moritz as he walked the whole length of the Icknield Way in 1913. In Buckland church, on the edge of Chiltern country, he found 'one of the most dismal certificates of life, marriage, motherhood, religion, death and the philosophy of relatives I have ever seen'. This was the memorial in the church to Frances Russell of Great Missenden reading, after the facts of her life including the loss of an infant and her age, 'The fleeting moments of prosperity, the tedious hours of Adversity, and the lingering illness which Providence allotted she bore with equanimity and Christian resignation. Reader go and do likewise.'

It must have been a strange walk, lasting as it did ten days and providing a book of 300 pages* full of delight and with nothing to say. All Thomas saw in Chinnor was the tablet to William Turner in the church pointing out that, 'here the wicked cease from troubling', as indeed they do, and the outside of the Bird in Hand. His morning pint he took at the Royal Oak where they complained about the heat; as they still would unless the temperature was half a dozen degrees below zero. No one feels the cold in the Chilterns, it is warmth which troubles them.

Thomas was determined on Ewelme and spent the preceding night at Watlington, thinking little of it, devoting ten pages to a description of the pictures on the walls of his bedroom. When he got to Ewelme he 'could not get into the church' and contented himself with more tombstone inscriptions. Yet this was a man who could not only see, but observe,

> *I like the dust on the nettles, never lost*
> *Except to prove the sweetness of a shower.*

* *The Icknield Way*, Constable, 1913.

Those contrasting extracts serve to pinpoint the Chilterns of the day before yesterday, yesterday, and today. Everyone remarks upon the emptiness, the aloofness of Chiltern churches. Yet Moritz fell in love with the church in Nettlebed which the soldiers who dined with him called a 'miserable place', and Thomas did not bother to have the door at Ewelme unlocked. He was young and for one year more able to laugh at tombstones. But his landlord at Watlington only charged him two shillings and gave him a special call at five a.m. And Moritz kept trying to go back to the White Hart at Nettlebed.

No one walks about today as did those two men, but in recent weeks Mr. Don Gresswell has revealed his plans for Chiltern networks which will give up to half a dozen footpath walks of 15 miles or so in length. It would still be an interesting experience to walk the Icknield Way, all in Chiltern country from Dunstable to Goring, but parts of it would be dangerous, and the difficulties of turning off here and there for today's high points of Chiltern beauty rather more pronounced than they were. There would be no dust on the roads, but plenty of the 'stink and insolence' which Thomas experienced from the primitive motor-cars and 'foreign-looking chauffeurs' of 1913.

This writer has just ceased to be 'foreign' after 21 years in the same Chiltern village, and with an experience of the whole area that began in 1940. It would be easy to write, 'Those were the days' and of course, looking backwards as a true Chiltern man should do, there are only golden days and scarlet sunsets to be recalled. One forgets the deep Chiltern snow of one's first arrival at one's Chiltern house, the furniture standing in a foot of it, the removal men shaking their heads as removal men always do and remarking as they looked disapprovingly at the low thatch and the tiny windows, 'None of it will go in'. Instead one remembers a first visit to Mr. Thomas's Bird in Hand (then kept by Mr. Harman) and the first remark of a Chiltern man in a strong Chiltern accent, so like the accent of South Norfolk as to be almost indistinguishable from it: 'You've come to live in a village where we like to live a long time. Let an old woman fall down a well round here and, if she's under ninety, we like to hold an inquest.' The very next year such an inquest was held, but now all the village is on mains of water and sewage, the old people are cut off from us in a settlement of their own, we are over-conscious of dirt, and inquests have become infrequent.

It is more than an education, it is a delight, to talk to an indigenous Chiltern man. He will know a great deal about answers to any questions you may be putting to him, but he will be slow to divulge them. He will be summing you up, judging how much importance you will attach to his comments, or how much you think you might be talking down to him, or feeling that you should be using simpler language. When he is satisfied on these matters and knows that you are a potential friend, you will begin to learn something about the Chilterns which is not in any of the books. You will discover, for an invented example, just why a particular incumbent is like the man in Nettlebed Mr. Moritz found so aloof, or perhaps why he is leaving the parish. The inventors of the English folk scene, Kipling in the 'Puck' volumes, Chesterton with his philosophy of the English mediaeval guilds, Belloc presenting his readers with a Sussex which never was (compare W. H. Hudson's *Nature in Downland*) should have come to the deep Chilterns for their silent Englishmen. But it was *terra incognita* in their day as in many respects it still is.

The favourite places become legion as the mind passes over 30 years. One develops a Chiltern sense, knowing what is bound to happen in a given village situation and who will soon not be talking to who as a result of that. One knows why a particular parochial church council is not after all going to put through a much trumpeted reform, why a certain parish council is losing three of its valued members, or, to mention specific examples of how things really work in England, the reasons behind the reasons which decided the Government against an airport at Wing, and were holding up the clearance of the dangerous corner at the Henton/Princes Risborough road junction. This sense grows more accurately selective with the years. One learns strange things about particular motor-car parks, or medical practices, or building plans. One learns why a housing development 20 miles away is going forward on land which was declared impossibly steep and unsuitable only 12 months earlier. One learns who is 'at the back of all that; but mind you I don't know anything really'. One of the most commonly heard Chiltern expressions is 'Mind you keep my name out of it; I don't want to get involved in anything.' Non-involvement is almost a religion in the Buckinghamshire and Oxfordshire Chilterns.

But despite the taciturn nature of the people, who are basically as warm-hearted as any in England, there is no lack of support in the area for the preservation and conservation societies which grow stronger each year. All of them, the Chiltern Society, the county branches of the Council for the Protection of Rural England, the various village societies such as the Chinnor and the Ewelme Societies, and, on the fringe, the powerful Friends of the Vale of Aylesbury, have enough members and enough keen observers and actual physical workers to ensure that all activities which, possibly essential, should yet be questioned (the digging of huge gravel pits, the pulling down of buildings having historical or architectural value, the closing of footpaths, the construction of new roads) are subjected to reasonable public discussion. These societies and associations engage also in valuable long-term projects; the restoration by the Chiltern Society of the smock mill at Lacey Green near Princes Risborough is a case in point, the securing for all time of the Chinnor Hill summit by the Oxfordshire, Berkshire and Buckinghamshire Natural History Society another.

Every Chiltern resident has his or her own personal, almost private 'Chilterns', and the various societies offer ways in which these may be preserved. Such a 'Chiltern Country' exists in the mind of this writer, and it might be of interest to look at it for a few pages, the reader all the time moving amendments or positively substituting a 'Chilterns' of his own.

There can be no argument about the heart of the Chilterns as a glance at the Ordnance map shows the town of High Wycombe almost exactly at the centre of the sheet. In every direction from that far-from-completely unlovely town something of beauty and value lies within a couple of miles. The conscious explorer will at once become aware of too much random or almost random overbuilding, but this is less noticeable to the sightseer on his way to a place or object. The National Trust village of West Wycombe, always beautiful, has again become almost peaceful now that three-quarters of the traffic has been drained off by a motorway. In 30 years there has been scarcely a change in the 'turn off' at this village for Bledlow Ridge, or in the lane up to the caves and church. There is a car park for the greatly increased numbers wishing to visit the various 'sights' but it is hardly noticeable. The steep grass gets worn in summer by innumerable children playing in safety, but the golden ball on the church still appears to rear itself out of solitude, and the view from the open spaces around the church seems unchanged.

The miles from the A40 to the top of Chinnor Hill are as rewarding as ever they were. There are considerably more houses on Bledlow Ridge than there were in the war years, but they have all or nearly all been sited with care. There are still long stretches of high open road with views to lift the heart.

The High Wycombe/Princes Risborough/Aylesbury road remains full of interest for itself alone. Motorists should stop more often than they do merely to look about them, and this is especially true in the Chilterns. It has been stressed more than once in this book that all the Chilterns have been designated an Area of Natural Beauty and a surprising number of districts have the additional distinction 'Great Natural Beauty'. Always this beauty is that of slope and trees, and it is thus confined and may be studied and enjoyed in exactly the same way as a great picture in a gallery. There are a score of places within ten minutes by car from High Wycombe quite unremarkable in themselves where the visitor at any time of year may sit at peace. Any direction will serve. High Wycombe to Amersham, to Bourne End and Maidenhead, through Loudwater to Burnham, the whole dense network of secondary roads and lanes towards Great Missenden, will produce moments of sheer pleasure.

There are two roads out of Oxford which provide memorable

Chiltern experiences: the old so-called 'coach road' through Stad-hampton to Watlington, the B480, which finds its way eventually to Henley, here and there becoming the Icknield Way, and on to Newbury. The other is the main Oxford/Dorchester/Wallingford road which displays the Oxfordshire Chiltern ridge to great advantage.

The secret Chilterns, the haunts of deer, the shy rarer birds, shielded from traffic by inaccessibility, are for genuine country lovers. They have nothing much to offer but solitude, a delight more difficult of attainment in England each year as more and more of us seek it out. Look for it in the Chilterns all round Checkendon and Stonor and Fawley. Go to Wormsley, walk away from the motor-cars on Watlington Hill, spend an hour at Jordans, or rest behind the church at Little Gaddesden. There is no fear that the mention of these places will flood them with visitors, there is nothing to do in them, they are mostly none too easy to find, it is better to leave the car and walk. You will never have much company on foot in the Chilterns.

On the road maps of the motoring organisations, or in the expensive productions to assist 'getting about' which are to be found in every modern motor-car, the Chilterns scarcely exist. The palm of a hand is enough to blot out the entire area. The place names are in small print and uninviting, there is nothing to say that Princes Risborough and Wendover are utterly different in size and character, that any motorist should pause in Amersham, but drive if possible briskly through, say, Berkhamsted. The church at Little Kimble is worth a drive of 100 miles, but thousands of motor-cars sweep past it all day long, all the year round, because it is perhaps 50 yards from the main road.

It is not the business of motoring bodies to set out the superb quality of the Little Kimble murals, but to print the name in black italic on the map to show that a reliable garage is there to be found. Ewelme, the Mecca of all Chiltern explorers, albeit at a limit of the territory, is shown in red italic; there is nothing about Ewelme in the text. Sheet 159 of the Ordnance Survey depicts everything in the area, the Roman and Saxon remains, the abandoned ruins, the march of the Icknield Way, the sprawl across the map of the Grimsditch, the sites of battlegrounds, the homes of our pit-delling forefathers. No Chiltern lover should be without this map. With its help he may now make the lamentable discovery that at long last Mr. Peel's famous remark about Dame Lys is no longer true. The wayfarer will now have difficulty in sitting there astride the Icknield Way from Wednesday until Tuesday without disturbance. An enterprise of pigs will claim his attention and their attendant lorries, tractors, delivery vans and collection trucks disrupt his train of thought. No matter : a thousand yards, or less, away he may still find the peace he wants.

There exists within the 500 square miles of the Chilterns proper, a large number of places which can only be described as part of an 'invented' Chilterns as they appear in such widely differing guises to different writers or speakers. Stevenson thought Wendover 'an ordinary sort of place' and Massingham did not disagree. But Miss Uttley came into Wendover at dusk and saw a girl at a window combing her hair by the light of a candle. Wendover could never be quite the same to Miss Uttley again, or to her readers. To this writer Stoke Poges is horrible, choked with traffic, and ill-mannered persons, utterly remote from the homespun philosophers of Gray's poem. Miss Uttley saw a tramp there with a carnation in his coat, and he was singing. That would have enabled her to look at the famous church with a clearer, happier, eye and to take in her hand a kindly and tolerant pen.

When Sir Niklaus Pevsner sees on his 'perambulations' a Dissenting chapel of some late eighteenth-century design, he may be physically and mentally disturbed. But Sir John Betjeman may feel uplifted : and this writer set off on a mental course which might include some generalisations about the effect of education on taste and how comparatively recently the people all about that chapel had learned to read. Such thoughts occur to him every day of the week as he passes the Chinnor Reading Room, recently mutilated architecturally by the addition, through noble voluntary effort, of two much-needed lavatories 'pinned' to the exterior; or the restored remains of the British School in Chinnor, now the headquarters of a revived and strengthened Silver Band. No writer from the earliest times has ever seen anything much in Chinnor. This one lives there and feels more a part of English History with the passage of every day. But a year ago there were five wooden headboards in Chinnor churchyard, now swept away in the proper interests of a better, cleaner, more cheerful area round the church. These things have to be, just as one of the handsomest buildings in Thame had recently to be demolished to provide a site for a Woolworth store. The building was unoccupied, could not be adapted, and is already forgotten.

Princes Risborough is a useful little shopping town with a new supermarket, or, according to mood, the former home of the Black Prince, and a village which almost certainly provided lodging for William the Conqueror. Take the Aylesbury road out of it and at once there is Monks Risborough, of great importance up to the Dissolution, and Whiteleaf, a main point for all Chiltern speculations. For some people all that is left of the Chilterns is in the mind. For them Princes Risborough should be a fine place for meditation.

At Jordans, fancy and reality join hands. Even on this side of the Atlantic the word 'Mayflower' is in the same magical group as Chimborazo and Cotopaxi, and to stand by Penn's grave looking at the barn and farmhouse, which employed Mayflower timbers in their building, is to summon up the Thirteen Colonies, the Old Dominion and the Daughters of the Revolution. And to one visitor at least thoughts of a country where not so long ago it was customary to revile the idea of Freedom of Conscience and to imprison the men and women who preached it. Thomas Ellwood, buried just behind William Penn, saw the inside of at least three Chiltern gaols.

The whole length of the Grimsditch and all the Icknield Way have aroused different emotions in different breasts. For instance Edward Thomas when he came to Wallingford along the Icknield Way from Ewelme, crossed the bridge and went into the private bar of the nearest inn to provide a setting for his thoughts on 'taproom' versus 'private bar' philosophy. But another writer might see, every time he crossed Wallingford Bridge, a vision of three knights 'clothed in snowy white' escorting Queen Matilda across the frozen Thames in December 1145 to make good her escape from Oxford (and King Stephen), to Abingdon, Wallingford, and the ultimate safety of Normandy.

So it is with Grimsditch. Many Chiltern writers prefer to ignore this immense artifact, others to indulge their fancy. But there are private persons, now, in the seventies of the twentieth century, who glance over their shoulders as they walk in strong sunlight along certain stretches of this ancient boundary. So much has happened in the Chilterns over so many centuries that the appearance of 'three misbegotten knaves in Kendal Green' could hardly cause surprise, and there are those who still look nervously for highwaymen in the neighbourhood of Turville Heath.

Massingham's true loves were not to be found in Buckinghamshire at all, but in the hidden depths of the Oxfordshire Chilterns and particularly at Berin's Hill and Maidensgrove. It is thought that Berin's Hill must be connected in some way with Bishop Birinius, a missionary from Pope Honorius 1st to the King of Wessex in 634. But all that country has the feel of great age and as if for hundreds of years time had slumbered and was only now awakening.

Few people actually walk the Chiltern Hills; they look at them or drive along those roads which cross them or follow the lines of the ridges. The high Chilterns are not much lower than the general run of the Malvern Hills, but lack the steepness of those 'real mountains', as Wilfrid Noyce once called them. But no real idea of Chiltern country can be obtained without one or two excursions of a mountaineering nature. It is after all not very difficult to walk up the lane marked 'Wainhill Only' just beyond Chinnor Village, or even to leave the Chinnor/High Wycombe road for a few hundred yards at the start of Bledlow Ridge. Great rewards await such adventurous behaviour. There is still a track by the Post Office at Chinnor, the Donkey Track, which is a pure country walk leading to delights. It is not yet 30 years since an elderly solicitor tested this writer's assertion on the Donkey Track that he would find it easier to walk uphill if he put his hands into his pockets and leaned forward. He became an enthusiast for hill walking.

How sad it is to come to the end of a Chiltern book and to feel as James Agate did when contemplating the nine volumes of his diary that he had 'written so much and said so little'. One takes a Chiltern index at random and runs through the place names. All one has said about Studham is that the church there is hideous and contains a Norman font. Yet a considerable chapter could be devoted to Studham. There was a hunting farmer there once, and a farming family which spread all over Bedfordshire, producing country solicitors and minor industrialists, and the worst farmer in England, who migrated to Great Missenden and nearly died of starvation and vexation on those hungry gravels.

And was enough said about the Italianate fittings in the church at Fawley and their connection with the great house of Chandos and the Knightly times of mediaeval England. Or of Hughenden which should be a place of pilgrimage for all who love England, not so much to see the Disraeli graves, or the house, which Pevsner found 'excruciating', but to reflect that the England we know today was produced by the man who lies there out of a still feudal country in which 80 per cent of the population had almost literally nothing.

Should more have been attempted about the Battle of Chalgrove Field; or the Civil War skirmish in Chinnor; or the Cromwellian thinking which put a man of these parts into prison for kissing his wife on a Sunday, but did nothing to the man (and there must have been hundreds of him), who knocked out the glass from most of the Chiltern church windows, destroyed the beautiful carvings which were thought of as detestable images, and, in fits of Christian zeal, pulled down from rood screens as many crosses as he could find?

Certainly there should have been more about the old Chiltern people, the families who have lived in the Chiltern villages for centuries, Clarkes, Mundays, Eggletons, Dodswells, Norths and, of course, Smiths, Browns and Robinsons. When Conan Doyle wrote *The Musgrave Ritual* did he know that there would almost certainly be one; or that the name is as familiar in parts of the Chilterns as Doyle is in Ireland? A visit to Sydenham, Henton, or Emmington, hamlets ranged about the parish of Chinnor, would have put him right. He would have found a spirit of caution in Chinnor itself, there is still a connection between the Church of St Andrew and the Musgrave family. Indeed it is not much more than a hundred years since a Musgrave was Rector of Chinnor, but, as Doctor Watson might have observed, 'the world is not yet ready for that story'.

How much of Chiltern lore and fact depends for its survival on continuance on the parish churches. What now could be said of Chenies apart from the Bedford monuments, or of Aldbury without the Pendley Chapel, or of Fingest without its bifurcated tower? Only at Ewelme are there buildings anywhere in the Chilterns (other than half a dozen great houses and only one of them, West Wycombe Park, in the highest class) to set descriptive pens flowing. But in almost every church there is a monument, a plaque, a brass or other beautiful object to set the imagination working and to animate the dust under the effigies of crusaders, or the calm faces of long dead mothers and children. In all the Chilterns there is perhaps only one spectacularly beautiful church, but there is not one without something of interest or devotion to give the visitor pause. Let no motorist be deterred from entering a Chiltern church by its all too obviously restored exterior; in most of them there is much to remind him of our long history.

Walk about in the little Chiltern towns. It is only the presence of parked cars in every inch of available space which creates everywhere the impression that today all towns are the same. They are not. High Wycombe on foot is an infinitely pleasanter place than High Wycombe as seen from a motor-car. Amersham on foot is delightful, and so is Wendover, and Great Missenden, and the old part of Beaconsfield, and Denham Village (almost unknown to the motorist) and Princes Risborough. In all these places (and here Aylesbury and Thame must be included), there are private houses and shops of great beauty to be seen, books and antiques to be bought, ancient pubs to be visited, the true harsh accent of the Chilterns to be heard.

The Chiltern winters are long, cold and hard, the climate producing the kind of men and women who may safely be entrusted with the preservation of our liberties. Not here in the Chilterns will juries first be abolished, as is now suggested, or planners and developers find everything easy and to their liking. Already on the new estates a strong spirit is emerging more than capable of defeating those who see a field as a land bank, or a tree as an obstacle. They have not been slow to learn, the newcomers to the Chilterns, that a Preservation Order may be granted for a tree as quickly as for a building. They mean to keep as much as possible of what they have bought for so high a price.

For land prices and house property values in the Chilterns are rocketing faster than elsewhere. Ten years ago a new small house on a High Wycombe development could be obtained for about £4,500. This was considered excessive and gave impetus to the development of estates around outlying villages where the better quality 'estate' houses could be run up for about £4,000. Both those prices have nearly doubled and for an old house standing in any sort of garden and with a little privacy the price is almost anything the owner cares to ask. For how long this will continue no one can say. On the edge of the Chilterns the new huge city of Milton Keynes will be emerging before long and maybe destroying for ever some aspects of the Vale of Aylesbury. It will be closer to all the work centres, except Oxford and High Wycombe, which now attract young couples to the Chilterns.

And there is no doubt that the general policy of the Department of the Environment is beginning to emerge and that it is a policy with teeth. More and more building must come in the Chilterns, but there is no need for overbuilding and the rushing up of hastily conceived schemes. Periods of rest and consolidation are now being enforced by the Department in those cases where populations have grown too fast for any sort of plans for the future to be arranged.

Some Afterthoughts

There are no signs at present that the Chilterns are to be invaded by the hordes of prospectors (there are said to be over 100 interested American companies), now searching England for oil, gold, zinc, lead, silver or anything else out of which there is money to be made. The ten National Parks are all under this threat but as yet this Area of Great Natural Beauty has been spared. An expert committee has recently suggested the clear felling of much beechwood and a replanting of mixed forest, conifers and hard woods combined. This may be good for the Chilterns eventually and it will take 50 years or more to alter to any extent the appearance of the more typical districts. But time presses for the publication of the Report on the Chilterns in preparation by the Chiltern Society. This may well prove to be the most important study of an English area ever made, thousands of people having provided individual answers to problems which have then been computerised into single possible solutions. It should be a fascinating document of immense value.

It has never been true anywhere that in the long run people get the kind of country they deserve; they get the kind of country imposed upon them by irresistible forces. London and the great Birmingham conurbation must continue to press against the Chilterns, but even another million families within the next 20 years could be comfortably absorbed if the pace is kept slow. If there is time to build the schools, to lay out spaces for recreation, to think about the roads before enlarging them or constructing new ones, and above all for the lessons of history to be studied. Eight years ago the railway from Princes Risborough to Thame was closed. Now with the rapid expansion of Thame it is to be re-opened. Before long there will be similar pressure to re-open the Watlington Line. In five years, perhaps less, as already suggested, private motoring may have to be banned in the interests of oil conservation. What happens then in remote Chiltern settlements? Children of ten will only be 15 then. How are they to get to school or their fathers to work? The return of steam and water transportation may be just round the corner.

164

Appendices

Notes on Chiltern Lollardy, the Chiltern Hundreds,
and present-day life in the area

Wycliffe was a Junior Fellow in Merton College, Oxford in 1356 and died in his bed, of a stroke, in 1384. He was not therefore in any sense a founder or even a precursor of the Reformation in England. What he, and especially his followers of long after his death wanted was the end of the Sacraments, marriage, other than by consent, font baptism and bell ringing. They wanted the Pope eliminated, of course, but also the kings who supported the Papacy. The martyrs of 1411 suffered for treason and heresy, not heresy alone. Protestantism, as such, was still unheard of.

In the Chilterns there has always been a Puritan tradition, of resistance to forms and ceremonies, and resistance to any form of human dominance. The views of Wycliffe found ready acceptance, taking shape as nonconformity long before the word was associated with specific kinds of belief.

Wycliffe had been dead for 80 years when James Willis, 'The Apostle of the Chilterns', began making converts in Henley, Marlow, Hambleden, Turville and Chinnor. He was a Bristol man, but his followers in the Chilterns were strong-minded and persistent, and their simple habits and beliefs flowered when official Nonconformity took shape in the seventeenth century. Poor Willis was brought to trial before Bishop Chedworth at Wooburn (Bucks) in August 1462. He made a formal abjuration in order to die a good Christian and thus was only hanged instead of being hanged and burned. Those were rough and bloody times.

Two years later Willis's disciple, William Aylward, was similarly condemned. Aylward was even more violent in his views than Willis, adding singing in church and the use of wind organs to the 'forms' he wanted abolished. His home was in Henley and his preaching influence wide in the Chilterns. We know nothing about him apart from his 'Confession', which described the Pope of the day as 'a great beast and a devil of hell and a synagogue'. He referred to the king, 'and all those who maintained the church' as hoping that they 'would go to the devil and in especial the king because of his great supportation of the church'. William Aylward's spirit lives on in the Chilterns, as for example in the Chinnor of today. An immediate complaint was made to the present Rector of Chinnor (Rev. R. Horner) within minutes of the first ringing of the newly dedicated peal of bells in the late summer of 1969.

Lollardism, or the nonconformity of the day, rather, went 'underground' in the Chilterns after the failure of the Oldcastle rising in 1411. Sir John Oldcastle was perhaps born 150 years too soon. He corresponded with Good King Wenceslas about the world struggle against anti-Christ; he was a supporter of Huss, the famous Bohemian heretic, and the prime mover in the Peasants' Revolt against king and Church. Only in East Anglia and the Chilterns was there any real support for the rising, a fact made abundantly clear in the endpaper maps of Mr. K. B. McFarlane's *John Wycliffe and English Nonconformity*. From the Chilterns an unarmed rabble set out for St. Giles Fields in London. We have no information about their numbers or names; only that parties of them came from Henley, Hambleden, Turville, Chinnor and Little Missenden; also from Beauchamp, Amersham and High Wycombe, and from Dunstable, Great Gaddesden, Bovingdon, Latimer, Chenies and the Chalfonts. They had support from the Cheyne family of Beauchamp Drayton (just outside the strict borders of Chiltern country), but these were alone among the gentry of the times in their Lollardry, appointing heretical incumbents to both Chenies and Drayton at the beginning of the fifteenth century. Three members of this family were implicated in Oldcastle's rising, one of them being killed or, more likely, executed. Of the rank and file killed, hanged and burned we know absolutely nothing, not even their names surviving their deeds. Of these Chiltern

26   *A wing of the superb West Wycombe Park*

men seven, we know, were burned and 31 hanged within days of their setting out. And that is all, except that every one of them lived within ten miles of High Wycombe.

The rising had no hope of success, the whole Establishment of the day was against them, and their deaths meant nothing to anyone except their wives and children, if they had wives and children. Even that we don't know. It is not reasonable to look for memorials to them in the Chiltern churches; they were opposed to any kind of organised church, any kind of ordained minister, all the Sacraments, any formal doctrines. They would have been just as violently opposed, as were their Puritan successors, to the Established Church which took shape from the Reformation. But they were Chiltern men; stubborn, ignorant perhaps, English to the core. Everything they did is forgotten now, and it was unimportant while they were doing it, except that they died for it. They were essentially the same men whose names appear on every memorial to two World Wars in every Chiltern village and on the wooden headboards or stones in every Chiltern churchyard. It is not difficult to find out what they were like. Call at any Chiltern cottage which is not shiny with new paint, has no concealed oil-tank for central heating, no double-glazing or adjacent garage for two cars. The occupant will then, most likely, have a Chiltern accent to go with his Chiltern name. He will keep his hat on his head; he will not ask you to step inside. He may well, in reply to your general inquiry about his way of life, invite you to mind your own business. He may add that he has no intention of getting mixed up in anything. One of his ancestors may well have been hanged or burned in St. Giles Fields in the cold winter of 1411.

THE CHILTERN HUNDREDS

One of the most commonly asked questions about the Chilterns is 'What exactly are The Chiltern Hundreds, and where are they?'

27 *At the edge of Ashridge with a view towards the Vale*

From time to time a notice appears in the papers that such and such a Member of Parliament has 'applied for the Chiltern Hundreds'. This means that for personal reasons he wishes to give up his seat during the life of a particular Parliament. In the ordinary way he is not allowed to do this, other than by being appointed to 'an office of profit under the Crown'.

For many centuries we have had in this country an excellent general practice of devising fictions in order to cope with exceptional or difficult circumstances. In great industries men who have been chairman are turned into presidents in order to remove from them the voting powers of the Board. Members of clubs and institutions are elected to unreal positions of honour for the same reasons; certain clerics are elevated to an agreed height, at which they are safely out of the way. Such an honourable fiction is the Stewardship of the Chiltern Hundreds. The Hundreds no longer exist, there is no Steward. If there were he would not be paid. But undoubtedly the Stewardship, if the Hundreds existed, would be held under the Crown, and, if it were paid would be an office of profit, not in any circumstances to be held by a Member of Parliament. It is therefore assumed that the Hundreds still exist, that Stewards may still be appointed, and that, in theory, they might still be paid. It follows that the appointment of a sitting Member of Parliament to such a post would automatically render his seat vacant, which it does.

At one time there were three Chiltern Hundreds, the Hundred of Desborough, the Hundred of Burnham, and the Hundred of Stoke. They were all in Buckinghamshire. In Saxon times the administrative unit in the country was a township, called, in the later Norman times, a manor. These were formed into Hundreds for purposes of judicial administration and defence, and many of them, which had been the property of Saxon kings, became the property of Norman sovereigns. They were managed by bailiffs or stewards. These usually farmed out their offices for a lump sum.

From the earliest Norman times the Hundreds had been in the hands of the King, but under the Cromwellian Commonwealth they were sold, reverting to the Crown at the Restoration. In 1679 they were leased to Thomas D'Oyley who may be said to be the last acting or practical Steward. After him the rents of the Hundreds were sold as free farm rents and all the duties and powers of Stewards came to an end.

The Stewardship of the Chiltern Hundreds, as a sinecure office, derives from an adaptation of the Place Act of 1708. This was intended to prevent the formation of a Court Party, committed to certain causes by the fruits of office, within the House of Commons itself.

This Place Act was, in fact, first cited for the convenience of a Member, Mr. John Pitt, who wished to change his constituency. He had no way of doing so, other than as the holder of an office of profit under the Crown, and he applied for the office of Stewardship of the Chiltern Hundreds, was awarded it, and passed into history. Nowadays the appointment is made by the Chancellor of the Exchequer; it is his business to see that any Member seeking release from his seat and duties is impelled by no dishonourable motive. The signing of the Warrant to the Stewardship automatically strikes the Member's name from the House of Commons list, and the document, when sent to the Member, does not bear the letters M.P. in the superscription.

The three Hundreds, while no longer existing, are clearly defined and still shown on maps of the area. The Thames forms one boundary, from Medmenham to beyond Eton and Datchet. The western line is marked by the River Coln, embracing Amersham, Chesham, and the Chalfonts. The third leg of the triangle of Hundreds follows the hills and ridges sheltering or exposing the typical Chiltern villages and townships from Hughenden and Bradenham, round by Saunderton and Radnage, to Turville and Ibstone.

Most of the information in this note is contained in *The Chiltern Hundreds*, by the Reverend Albert J. Foster, M.A., published in 1897 as one of the fruits of covering every square mile of the territory, note and sketch books in hand.

Appendices

PRESENT-DAY LIFE IN THE CHILTERNS

Only 20 years ago a man living in an 'outer' Chiltern village, that is anywhere beyond the southern escarpment of 'Metroland', would, if he worked in London, have had to spend at least three hours a day in trains. As recently as 1950 the private motor-car was still largely a pleasure vehicle, and it was not until after 1955 that the entire country began to adapt itself with frightening speed to a new way of life in which the motor-car is an essential of existence, almost a carapace.

Nowadays Chiltern man has a number of options. He can drive himself to and from London every day, as thousands do. He can drive or be driven by his wife to any of the few Chiltern main line stations and enjoy a comfortable service of non-stop trains. And he need no longer work in London as an essential in the process of 'getting on'. There is every kind of work in the surrounding towns, and a hundred miles of motoring a day is nothing to a modern young husband. Moreover he need no longer think of himself as a Chiltern man, and he does not.

Within living memory primary education in the Chilterns was a matter of reading, writing and arithmetic and fitting boys and girls to occupy what was called their proper stations in life. This meant local work in the Chiltern trades for the boys and domestic service for the girls. Here and there an exceptional boy or girl emerged from the ruck, but any photograph of primary school children taken anywhere in the Chilterns at the turn of the century will convey exactly what was going on. Only 30 years earlier a Chiltern farmer was complaining at his parish council of a schoolteacher who was pinning crude educational pictures to the school walls instead of concentrating the minds of her pupils on the use of the fork, the mattock and the hoe. Fathers lived within walking distance of their work in those days; mothers, trained in the domestic arts by their hard early lives as servants, kept ducks and made lace. The bicycle changed some of that. It was a fast, ultra-modern form of transportation and new mass-production methods soon brought it within the reach of those who were still called 'the poor'. The bicycle set fresh limits to the work circle. It became possible for a man to seek work within a radius of 10 to 15 miles. But essentially the life pattern of the Chiltern villages was unchanged by the bicycle. It has been almost ended by the motor-car.

The population explosion into the Chilterns is not a matter for despair, but already large areas have been scarred beyond hope of redemption by the avariciousness of 'developers'. And even in the best-planned Chiltern developments some obvious facts appear to have been overlooked. A young couple entering with joy and enthusiasm their mortgaged estate house are going to fill it with children, particularly in a Welfare State which sets no upper limit to the size of families. There will thus be many Chiltern districts in the next 10 to 15 years facing the most serious problems of an educational, recreational, and occupational nature. Already parish and district councillors, parish clergy, school managers and teachers, all kinds of voluntary workers, together with doctors, nurses, and other official personages are at their wits' end as they contemplate desperately overcrowded schools, unforeseen water shortages, totally inadequate sewage schemes, dwindling public transport (killed by the ubiquitous private motor-car), and the now dangerously overcrowded approach roads to the villages. By 1980 there will be a whole new generation of Chiltern teenagers for whom no provision whatsoever has as yet been made. Time is running out.

Of course the problem of creating homes out of houses is everywhere being tackled. The estate gardens are beginning to be filled with trees and roses and flowering shrubs, uphill work on the stiff Chiltern clays overlying the chalk. But this will avail nothing if, just as the new families are settling down, just as the local and county authorities are getting on top of the educational and other problems, more big money continues to win against reason and the sensible aims of 'filling in', 'keeping within the parish line', and 'the preservation of the environment'. If that happens the steep hills of the Chilterns will no longer set limits to expansions, nor will the thought (already discussed learnedly in Chiltern publications), of 'economic pram mileage' and 'negotiable pram gradients', nonsense phrases to a planner in an office set beside a city pavement, deter the men who think in their own jargon of 'house densities per acre', 'land banks for development', and call men and women 'units'.

Ten years ago the word 'conservation' had no real meaning for ordinary people living in the Chiltern communities, but now conservation is a visible aim almost everywhere. As recently as 1940 Massingham despaired on nearly every page of *Chiltern Country*. He thought and wrote that nothing of interest or beauty could survive in the Chilterns for more than a couple of decades at the most. Nothing that was being done was right, nothing was going well or could go well. What man left uninjured, Massingham wrote, his machines would eliminate. He was not content to sound a note of warning; he blew a trumpet of doom. Yet among the things he knew, and loved so well, nearly all remain.

The present-day Chiltern dweller will not see horses working in the fields, or men with scythes. It is a long time since anyone came upon a properly constructed rick of sheaved corn, or loose hay. These things belonged to a time of low wages, not to a period in which the most expensive item everywhere in the world is the hand labour of craftsmen. The production of food at a price people will pay needs all the artifacts and chemicals Massingham so greatly deplored. There was no prettier sight up to and including the time of the Second World War than a line of women hand-pulling weeds across a field, but all the women and children in a parish could not perform the day's work of an intelligent man on a tractor fitted with a spraying machine. And the spraying machine does a better job, permanently and at half the price. Soon it will be doing it harmlessly as well.

Almost a million people have come to the Chilterns since Massingham wrote his book, lured in by the motor-car and comparatively cheap land rather than by the thought and expectation of country pleasures. But a note of this kind is not the place for a diatribe against a world phenomenon which is destroying the environment and building up cancerous diseases from Alaska to the Falkland Islands, which is killing and maiming hundreds of thousands of people every year, and which must be radically transformed within the next 10 to 15 years if any of us are to survive. And so far, and for the next few years, a man and woman living in the Chilterns can have a decent house and bring up a family with deep and peaceful countryside not far away. Above every town and village in the outer Chilterns there are still thick, quiet beechwoods, and lanes about green fields.

The current difficulties in the Chilterns are not new, only more intense, more widely spread. There were similar or related troubles in the past. The big churches would attract town dwellers; let them be closed; or let them fall down rather than that a village should be saddled with the crippling handicap of a restoration fund. Landowners were calling for pounds of flesh, much as they do today. There were fever districts here in the Chilterns; it was dangerous to visit the outskirts of Reading for example. There were stagnant ponds, gangs of ruffians, dens of iniquity. There were beer houses in which murders were plotted, and poachers who would shoot to kill. Strong efforts by the same sort of strong-minded people who chose the present-day Chilterns as their living place solved all those problems and many more. Our present discontents occasionally seem insuperable, but they are not. Life can still be more pleasant in the Chilterns, but we must 'look to our moat'. In the Middle Ages man had done nothing much in the way of technological development to think himself in danger, as we do now, from self-poisoning of the environment. Yet the Black Death crept over the known world, depopulating vast areas of Europe, and these islands. Much later London was decimated by plague, and twice in 300 years has been cleared by fire. There are more ways in Nature of controlling excess populations than by atomic bombs and nerve gases. But in the Chilterns, as everywhere else, we have only to take care of what we have, to be sure that it will survive us.

CHAPTER SEVENTEEN

A Short Chiltern
Bibliography with Notes

1. *Chiltern Country*, by H. J. Massingham.

Originally published in 1940 and out of date now, but still a delightful book, full of prejudice, highly coloured, despairing. Massingham thought the whole Chiltern area was finished, that there would be nothing but houses and horrors within ten years, that machines would destroy both agriculture and the people. He loathed anything new and on every page is at his most wrong when at his most vehement. It is a dangerous book to open; it cannot be put down.

2. *Chiltern Footpaths* and *Portrait of the Chilterns*. Both by Annan Dickson.

Indispensable for getting the 'feel' of the territory. Some interesting theories, too, notably suggestions about the earliest days of the Upper Icknield Way.

3. *The Chilterns* and *Discovering the Chilterns*. Both by J. H. B. Peel.

It is from *The Chilterns* that everyone quotes the lines about sitting on the Icknield Way at Dame Lys from Wednesday to Tuesday and never having to get out of the way of a motor-car. The little book, *Discovering the Chilterns* can be finished in an hour, leaving the reader with a very good idea of the whole 500 Chiltern square miles. For good measure there are a couple of pages on how to look round a church, any church.

4. *Story of the Chiltern Heathlands,* by J. H. Baker.
The developments in the heathland areas of the Chilterns have left this interesting out-of-print work sadly out-of-date. But works of this kind will eventually be all we have left to tell us about Goring Heath and similar places soon to be engulfed.

5. *The Chiltern Hundreds,* by Rev. A. J. Foster.
A truly remarkable work, dating from the turn of the century. Mr. Foster, who was vicar of Wooton in Bedfordshire, had set his foot on every square mile of the Chilterns before he began to write his little book. In addition to a full explanation of the origin of the Chiltern Hundreds there are scores of Chiltern anecdotes, each one delightfully 'glossed' with the wry comments of the author.

6. *The Bucks Explorer,* by Kate Bergamer.
A tiny book packed with interesting matter, most of it about artifacts and curiosities in the Chilterns. There is scarcely an oddity or curiosity in the Chilterns of Buckinghamshire which Miss Bergamer has left unnoticed and unillustrated.

7. *Buckinghamshire,* by Sir Niklaus Pevsner.
A volume in the Buildings of England series and indispensable to any serious Chiltern visitor, which is why it is made to fit the pocket. The book is strictly factual and highly condensed. It is only occasionally that Sir Niklaus 'lets himself go', but the whole small page lights up when he does. Of Hughenden Manor, for example; 'Lamb's details are excruciating ... the window-heads indescribable'. Of the Primitive Methodist Chapel in Stoken-church: 'A hideous-looking building in a belated and debased Italianate. The central window is particularly hard to appreciate.'

8. Roscoe's *Buckinghamshire,* revised by R. L. P. Jowitt and E. Clive Rouse.

The edition of 1950, the original being published in 'The Little Guides' series in 1900, has all the information any non-specialist could want about the flowers, animals and buildings of the County, principally of course in the Chilterns. Sound antiquarianism, with some excellent and forceful opinions, some of them political.

9. *Discovering Buckinghamshire*, by Cadbury Lamb.
Full of general information but with a more than useful set of indications about public houses in the area together with other places of refreshment.

10. *Buckinghamshire*, Official Handbook.
Devotes several pages of compressed information to the Chiltern area of the county. Does justice to the beauties of the country behind Bledlow Ridge, an almost forgotten enclave.

11. *Murray's Guide to Buckinghamshire*, by John Betjeman and John Piper.
Mainly a picture book, with a bleak text often a trifle quick in damning the hands of restorers. Like Massingham, Betjeman finds much that is new intrinsically offensive.

12. *Chiltern Country by Car*, by Peter and Helen Titchmarsh.
An excellent motoring guide to all the Chiltern country. The work of map reading and route finding has been done, and nearly every 'sight' worth seeing mentioned. A 'must' for the map pocket of any car touring the Chilterns.

13. *The Chilterns*, by Professor J. T. Coppock.
A comprehensive distillation of the entire area from maps. There are not 40 pages in this brochure, but it is a wonderful little book with more solid information to the page than could possibly be expected. The photographs, admirable in themselves, are there to explain and instruct. More than any other book about the Chilterns this one brings prehistoric Chiltern man to life,

going about his business on the banks of a forgotten Thames.

14. *Buckinghamshire*, by Alison Uttley.
   Not to be missed, because all the information is there. But Miss Uttley's pages are over decorated, straining credulity.

15. The 'Victoria' County History of England: The *Oxfordshire Volumes*.
   Nothing is omitted, from the names and ages of all the bells in all the churches, to the names and dates of all the buildings in all the villages. The debt is great but so is the labour of reading in these volumes enormous. For the specialist.

16. Miscellaneous Leaflets, Brochures, and occasional publications.
   All the Newsletters, Reprints, and Information Sheets of the Chiltern Society; all the Notes for worshippers and visitors to be found in nearly every Chiltern Church; specialised leaflets; the Picture Gallery at Cookham; detailed accounts of churches in connection with special functions, *Son et Lumière* and the like; Local information, (*A History of Jordans*, by Miss Anna Littleboy), sundry parochial records, the leaflets of urban councils; Specialised reading (Sir Laurence Weaver's *High Wycombe Furniture*); relevant book reviews often leading to newspaper correspondence and articles, viz 'The View over Atlantis' and subsequent speculations (in *The Listener*), about megalithic man and Straight Tracks in the Chilterns; photostats of material, i.e. Camden's *Britannia* on Buckinghamshire.

Index

References in italic type are to illustrations

Index

Index